Bob Thonen
The Church in Cleveland

6.00

Life-Study
of
Galatians

Messages 1-24

Witness Lee

Living Stream Ministry
Anaheim, California

First Edition, 1,000 copies. September 1990.

Library of Congress Catalog
Card Number: 84-80717

ISBN 0-87083-145-3

Published by

Living Stream Ministry
1853 W. Ball Road, Anaheim, CA 92804 U.S.A.
P. O. Box 2121, Anaheim, CA 92814 U.S.A.

Printed in the United States of America

CONTENTS

iv

xi

LIFE-STUDY OF GALATIANS

MESSAGE ONE

THE BACKGROUND AND SUBJECT
OF THE BOOK

Scripture Reading: Gal. 1:1-7; 3:1, 3; 4:17, 21; 5:2, 4; 6:12, 15

The books of Galatians, Ephesians, Philippians, and Colossians form a cluster of Epistles which make up the heart of the divine revelation in the New Testament. Therefore, these books are very important. Ephesians covers the church as the Body of Christ, whereas Colossians deals with Christ as the Head of the Body. Galatians is concerned with Christ, and Philippians, with the experience of Christ. In Colossians and Ephesians we receive a clear view of the Head and the Body. In Galatians and Philippians we see Christ and the experience of Christ.

Just as there are four seasons in the year, so there are seasons in our Christian experience. This means that in our experience with the Lord we pass through winter as well as summer. The winter experiences are helpful, for they prepare us for a new beginning, which comes in the spring. During the winter season the various kinds of life are reduced. Through the reduction that takes place in winter, life is prepared to grow again. Because in our spiritual experience there is the need for us to be reduced, we must be ready for winter at the appointed time. We may say that Galatians is a winter book, a book that reduces us and eliminates everything that should not be permanent. However, this reduction serves a very positive purpose: it prepares us for further growth in life.

We all need to be reduced. We need to be reduced not only in things that are natural or worldly, but even in the various aspects of our spiritual experience. For the sake of further growth in the Lord, we need to be reduced. Certain things in our Christian life may be very good, scriptural, and spiritual. But as long as these things are not Christ Himself directly, they should not be given a place with us very long. Only Christ Himself should have a permanent place in our Christian life. All other things, even the most spiritual experiences, must be reduced. In order for this reduction to take place, God ordains winter. We should never expect to have an endless summer in the Christian life. On the contrary, we should expect the recurring cycle of spring, summer, autumn, and winter. Whenever we come to a winter in our experience with the Lord, we should be encouraged that spring and summer will follow in due time. Therefore, we should be encouraged to be reduced in order to have another new beginning. It is my hope that these messages on Galatians will serve this purpose.

I. THE BACKGROUND

In order to study the book of Galatians properly, it is important to know the background and the subject of this book. All the books in the New Testament have a particular background. We thank the Lord for these backgrounds, even though, for the most part, they were not very positive. The Lord uses the negative background as a basis for the release of the divine revelation. The more negative a certain background is, the greater is the opportunity for the Lord to release His revelation. The worse the background, the greater is the need for God's revelation. If we see this, we shall thank the Lord for all the negative backgrounds that made it necessary for the books in the New Testament to be written.

The Gospel of John is a good example of a New Testament book written against a negative background. This Gospel was written during the last decade of the first century. At that time there was a tendency, even among Christians, to deny the deity of Christ. Some were doubting Christ's deity, and others were even denying this truth.

With such a trend as the background, this Gospel was written by the Apostle John. Without this Gospel, we could not have an adequate understanding of Christ's deity and His eternal existence. Neither could we realize how Christ could become our life. But through the Gospel of John we clearly see that Christ's deity is eternal and absolute. In this Gospel we also have the clear view of eternal life and of how Christ can be life to us. If there had not been such a dark background at the end of the first century, this wonderful Gospel probably would not have been written.

The Epistles of Paul were also written according to certain backgrounds. First Corinthians, for example, was written because of the confusion and divisiveness in the church at Corinth. If we did not have the book of 1 Corinthians, we would not know how Christ could be our enjoyment in all kinds of situations. This book describes the enjoyment of Christ in a way not found elsewhere in the New Testament. We should thank the Lord for the confusion in Corinth that gave rise to this Epistle.

The book of Colossians was also written according to a particular background, the background of the culture that had invaded the church at Colosse. With this cultural invasion as the background, the marvelous book of Colossians was written. Without that background, we would not have this book today.

In the same principle, the recovery of justification by faith at the time of the Reformation came forth out of a negative situation and a dark background. Apart from such a situation and background, the truth of justification by faith would not be as clear as it is today. This truth can no longer be blurred because the dark background causes it to stand out so definitely.

Now we come to the background of the book of Galatians. Written before A.D. 60, Galatians is earlier than either Ephesians or Colossians. Galatians was written in the earlier part of Paul's ministry, before he was imprisoned.

In order to have the proper experience of the church as

the Body of Christ, we need the book of Galatians. We need
both an adequate experience and understanding of all that
is conveyed to us in this Epistle. If we intend to practice
the church life today, we need to know the Christ revealed
in Galatians.

Galatians reveals that Christ is versus religion with its
law. The law given by God through Moses was the foundation of the Jewish religion. Judaism was built on the law.
The book of Galatians reveals that the very Christ whom
we need for the church life is versus law and religion.

A. The Churches in Galatia
Bewitched by the Judaizers

In verse 2 Paul speaks of "the churches of Galatia," a
province of the ancient Roman Empire. Through Paul's
preaching ministry, churches were established in a number of cities in that province. Hence, "churches," not
"church," is used when the apostle refers to them.

The churches in Galatia had been bewitched by the
Judaizers (3:1). They had been distracted from Christ to
Judaism. A good number of the New Testament believers
in the churches of Galatia had turned back to the old Jewish religion and were endeavoring to keep the law with the
ordinance of circumcision. This was the background that
gave Paul the opportunity to write this wonderful book.

In writing to the Galatians, Paul was very frank and
straightforward; he was not in the least political. For example, he called those Judaizers who were troubling the
Galatians "false brothers" (2:4). The Galatian believers
had been bewitched by these false brothers.

B. The Churches in Galatia Distracted
from Christ to Law

In 1:6 and 7 Paul says, "I marvel that you are so quickly
removing from Him Who has called you in the grace of
Christ to a different gospel, which is not another; only
there are some who trouble you and desire to pervert the

gospel of Christ." Here Paul comes to his subject. Because the churches in Galatia were deserting the grace of Christ and backsliding to the observance of the law, Paul was burdened to write this Epistle. The "different gospel" mentioned in verse 6 denotes the Judaistic observance of the law. The grace of Christ is versus the law of Moses (John 1:17). The Judaizers troubled the churches by perverting the gospel of Christ, or distorting it, thus misleading the believers, taking them back to the law of Moses. However, the observance of the law could never be a gospel that sets free the sinners under its bondage and brings them into the enjoyment of God. It could only keep them as slaves under its bondage.

1. Brought to Nought from Christ

Because they were distracted from Christ to law, the Galatians were being brought to nought from Christ (5:4). To be brought to nought is to be brought to nothing. In His salvation God has brought us into Christ and has made Christ to be profitable to us in every way. In His redemption God has placed us into His Son who is now everything to us. But the Judaizers had caused the Galatian believers to be distracted from Christ to the law. By turning from Christ to the law, the Galatians were being brought to nothing from Christ. According to the King James Version, Paul said to the Galatians, "Christ is become of no effect unto you." The Galatians were in a situation where the profitable Christ was of no effect to them. They were being deprived of all the profit that is in Christ and were separated from Him as a result. As the American Standard Version says, they were "severed from Christ."

2. Fallen from Grace

In 5:4 Paul also told the Galatians that they had "fallen from grace." To be brought to nought from Christ is to fall from grace. This implies that Christ Himself is the very grace, and that we, the believers, are in Him as grace. The profitable Christ is grace to us. To be severed from Him is to be fallen from grace.

3. To Be Justified by Law

In 5:4 Paul also points out that the Galatians were seeking to be justified by law. Although they had been justified in Christ, they had gone back to keeping the law and were trying to be justified by the works of the law. What a devilish subtlety! Fallen man cannot be justified before God by keeping the law. The only way to be justified is by faith in Christ, by believing in the Lord Jesus. Nevertheless, the Galatian believers had been bewitched and therefore were trying to keep the law. They were endeavoring to be justified and to please God by their own works.

4. To Practice Circumcision

The Judaizers were also constraining the Galatians to practice circumcision (6:12, 15). In Genesis 17 God commanded Abraham and his male descendants to be circumcised. Any male who refused to be circumcised was to be cut off from God's people. Circumcision, however, was simply a type of the crucifixion of Christ. The true circumcision that cuts off the flesh is not the circumcision practiced in the Old Testament; it is the crucifixion of Christ. Our flesh can be dealt with only by the cross of Christ. Christ's crucifixion was the fulfillment of the type of circumcision. Since we have the reality of circumcision, there is no longer the need for the shadow. Nevertheless, the Judaizers turned the Galatian believers from the reality back to the shadow. How foolish!

5. To Be Perfected by the Flesh

Furthermore, the Galatians were trying to be perfected by the flesh (3:3). This means that the Galatians were trying to perfect themselves through their own effort, through the works of the flesh, in which there is nothing good. How foolish the Galatians were!

II. THE SUBJECT

A. To Rescue the Distracted Believers
out of the Evil Religious Age

The subject of the book of Galatians is related to its background. The subject is the rescue of the distracted believers out of the evil religious age. In 1:4 Paul says that Christ "gave Himself for our sins, that He might rescue us out of the present evil age, according to the will of our God and Father." An age is a part of the world as the satanic system. An age refers to a section, an aspect, the present or modern appearance, of the system of Satan, which is used by him to usurp and occupy people and keep them away from God and His purpose. We may regard each decade as a distinct age or section of Satan's world system.

The various ages of the satanic system are expressed in the fashions of clothing that prevail during a certain period of time. For example, in the 1950s men's neckties were narrow, but in the late 1960s and throughout most of the 1970s, they were broad. Now, according to the latest change of style, they have become somewhat narrow again.

When I was young, I worked in a factory where hair nets were manufactured for export to the West. At first, the hair nets were large, designed to fit over hair styled in the shape of a tower. Then, to my surprise, we began to receive orders for small hair nets. The reason for the change was that women in the West were now wearing their hair very short, in a bobbed style, and therefore wanted small hair nets. By these illustrations of neckties and hair nets we can see that the world system of Satan has different ages, different sections.

The present evil age in 1:4, according to the context of this book, refers to the religious world, the religious course of the world, the Jewish religion. This is confirmed by 6:14-15, where circumcision is considered a part of the world — the religious world which to the Apostle Paul is crucified. Here the apostle emphasizes that the purpose of Christ's giving Himself for our sins was to rescue us, to pluck us

out, from the Jewish religion, the present evil age. This is
to release God's chosen people from the custody of the law
(3:23), to bring them out of the sheepfold (John 10:1, 3),
according to the will of God. Thus, in his opening word,
Paul indicates what he is about to deal with. He desires to
rescue the churches which were distracted by Judaism
with its law and to bring them back to the grace of the
gospel.

For years I was fond of 1:4 and used this verse in
messages. However, I did not realize that the present evil
age in this verse refers to the Jewish religion. At the time of
Paul, Judaism was very prevailing. His intention in writing to the Galatians was to rescue the distracted believers
from the tyranny of the present evil religious age.

In 1:4 Paul points out that in order to rescue us from the
present evil religious age Christ gave Himself for our sins.
This indicates that Christ died in order to rescue us from
Judaism. In John 10 we see that Christ as the good
Shepherd entered into the fold in order to bring His sheep
out of the fold and into the pasture. The fold in John 10
signifies the law or Judaism as the religion of the law, in
which God's chosen people were kept and guarded in
custody or ward until Christ came. Before the coming of
Christ, God used Judaism as a fold to keep His sheep. But
Christ has come as the Shepherd to bring the sheep out of
that fold to the pasture where they may feed on His riches.
Although Christ came to release the sheep from the fold,
the Judaizers crucified this good Shepherd. He died on the
cross not only for the sins of the sheep, but also to bring
them out of the fold.

According to the New Testament, the death of Christ
on the cross accomplished many things. In Ephesians 2 we
see that He gave Himself in order to abolish the ordinances for the creation of the one new man. In Galatians 1
we see that Christ gave Himself for our sins for the purpose
of rescuing us out of religion, out of the present evil age.

We should apply 1:4 not only to the Galatian believers,
but also to today's believers in Christ. Most Christians are

held in some kind of religious fold. Although in the New Testament the term fold is not positive (according to the Greek, the second occurrence of "fold" in KJV of John 10:16 should be "flock"), certain Christian hymns speak of being brought back to the fold in some kind of positive sense. We have pointed out that in John 10 the fold denotes Judaism. In principle, Catholicism and all the denominations are folds. Only the church is God's flock. Christ has brought us back to the flock, not to the fold. Many of us can testify that we have been rescued out of the fold and brought back to God's flock.

At the time of John 10, God's people, His sheep, were in the fold of Judaism. But as this chapter makes clear, Christ came to bring His sheep out of the fold and to form them with the Gentile believers into one flock, the church (10:16). Hence, the fold is religion, whereas the flock is the church. Today Catholicism and the denominations are folds that keep Christ's sheep. But Christ is seeking to rescue His sheep out of the various religious folds and to bring them together as the one flock.

Christ's death on the cross to deliver us from the present evil age was according to the will of God, the Father. To rescue the sheep from the fold is thus according to the will of God. Because Catholicism and the denominations damage the flock of God, they are opposed to the will of God. By building up their folds, they spoil the church life.

Today the Lord is still endeavoring to bring His sheep out of the fold. For this reason, a warfare is raging between religion and the Lord's recovery. The Lord Jesus came not to steal the sheep, but to lead the sheep out of the fold. The Judaizers, however, regarded Him as a sheep-stealer. In like manner, we in the Lord's recovery are accused of proselytizing, of stealing sheep. Although we do not proselytize, we do desire that the Lord's sheep may be led out of the fold and into the flock.

The Lord Jesus came into the fold, opened the door, and led the sheep out of the fold. The Judaizers crucified

Him. But through His death on the cross, the Lord gave Himself for our sins in order to rescue us from the religious fold. The principle is the same both with the believers in Paul's time and with us today.

B. Paul Becoming an Apostle

In 1:1 Paul speaks of his apostleship: "Paul, an apostle, not from men nor through man, but through Jesus Christ and God the Father, Who raised Him from among the dead." Paul's apostleship had much to do with the gospel he preached. The purpose of the book of Galatians is to let those who receive it know that the gospel preached by the Apostle Paul was not from man's teaching (1:11), but from God's revelation. Hence, at the very opening of this book, Paul emphasized the fact that he became an apostle not from men nor through man, but through Christ and God.

In verse 1, as in the entire book, Paul is careful in his use of words. Firstly he says that he did not become an apostle "from men"; he goes on to say that his apostleship was not "through man." He was made an apostle directly through Jesus Christ and God the Father, who raised Christ from among the dead. The law dealt with man as the old creation, whereas the gospel makes man the new creation in resurrection. God made Paul an apostle not according to his natural man in the old creation by the law, but according to his regenerated man in the new creation through the resurrection of Christ. Hence, Paul does not say here, "God the Father who gave the law through Moses"; he says, "God the Father who raised Christ from among the dead." God's New Testament economy is not with man in the old creation, but with man in the new creation through the resurrection of Christ. Paul's apostleship belonged altogether to the new creation, which transpires in our spirit through regeneration by the Spirit of God.

In verse 2 Paul goes on to speak of all the brothers who are with him. This indicates that he takes the brothers with him as co-writers to be a testimony and a confirmation of what he writes in this Epistle.

C. Grace and Peace to the Churches from God the Father and the Lord Jesus Christ

In verse 3 Paul says, "Grace to you and peace from God our Father and our Lord Jesus Christ." Grace is God as our enjoyment (John 1:17; 1 Cor. 15:10), and peace is the condition, the issue, which results from grace. Peace is the result of the enjoyment of God our Father. How good it is that grace and peace come to the churches from God our Father and from our Lord Jesus Christ!

LIFE-STUDY OF GALATIANS

THE APOSTLE'S GOSPEL

Scripture Reading: Gal. 1:6-12

In this message we come to 1:6-12. The main item revealed in these verses is the gospel preached by the Apostle Paul.

Many Christians think that the gospel has only one aspect. According to this concept, the message of the gospel is that we were sinners and that Jesus Christ, the Son of God, was incarnated and died on the cross for our sins so that we might be forgiven and saved. Although this is not wrong, it by no means includes all the aspects of the gospel found in the New Testament. In Matthew, Mark, Luke, and John, we have different aspects of the gospel. In the Acts we do not see one particular aspect. Instead, there are verses that refer to the aspects of the gospel presented in Matthew, Mark, Luke, and John. However, in all the Epistles written by Paul, Romans through Hebrews, we see a particular aspect of the gospel. We may call these Epistles the gospel according to Paul, or the fifth gospel.

Let us now consider the various aspects of the five gospels in the New Testament. Matthew reveals that Christ, the Son of David, came as the King to establish the kingdom of the heavens on earth. Hence, in Matthew the term, "the gospel of the kingdom," is used. Therefore, the aspect of the gospel emphasized in Matthew is that of the kingdom. The goal of this aspect of the gospel is to bring people into the kingdom.

The Gospel of John emphasizes eternal life. In this Gospel we see that from eternity Christ is the very Word of God, even God Himself. One day, the Word was incarnated (1:14). Furthermore, He died on the cross not only to redeem us from sin, but also to release the divine life so that He may impart Himself into us as eternal life. In this Gospel John brings us to a full realization of the divine life. For this reason, the Gospel of John may be called the gospel of life.

The aspect of the gospel emphasized in Luke is that of the forgiveness of sins. Here we find a record of how Christ came as a man to be our Savior, how He died on the cross to accomplish redemption and to solve the problem of sin so that we may be forgiven. According to Luke 24:47, repentance and forgiveness of sins should be preached in the name of Christ among all nations.

We have pointed out that Matthew is the gospel of the kingdom, that John is the gospel of life, and that Luke is the gospel of forgiveness. But what aspect of the gospel is emphasized in Mark? Mark is the gospel of service. According to this Gospel, Christ came as a slave to serve God by caring for God's people. Christ came, not to be ministered unto, but to minister, to serve (10:45). He came not only as the King to establish the kingdom, as the eternal One to impart life, and as the Savior to forgive the sins of those who believe in Him; He also came as a slave to serve God by ministering to His redeemed people. Thus, Mark emphasizes service.

Paul's gospel includes all the aspects of the first four Gospels. In his writings Paul speaks of the kingdom, life, forgiveness, and service. However, in his Epistles he covers much more. In Colossians 1:25 Paul says that he became a minister according to the stewardship of God to complete the word of God. Hence, Paul's gospel is the gospel of completion. Without Paul's gospel, the revelation of the gospel in the New Testament would not be complete.

Many important aspects of the gospel are found only in the writings of Paul. For example, in Colossians 1:27 Paul says that Christ in us is the hope of glory. Such a word cannot be found in the four Gospels, nor in the Epistles written by Peter or John. Mark may be regarded as Peter's spiritual son (1 Pet. 5:13), and he drew upon Peter as the source for much of the material in his Gospel. However, Mark says nothing about the indwelling Christ as our hope of glory. From Paul's gospel we learn that the Spirit of Christ is a seal and a pledge (Eph. 1:13-14). Although John speaks of the Spirit, he does not use the same terms Paul does. In Galatians 1:15 and 16 Paul tells us that it pleased God to reveal His Son in him. Such a word is not to be found in Matthew, Mark, Luke, or John. Paul also speaks of Christ living in us (2:20), of Christ being formed in us (4:19), and of Christ making His home in us (Eph. 3:17). Statements like these are not found in the four Gospels. Furthermore, in Ephesians 3:19 Paul speaks of being filled unto all the fullness of God. Matthew, Mark, Luke, and John have nothing to say about this.

In his Epistles Paul also tells us that we are members of the Body of Christ. He speaks of Christ as the Head and of the church as the Body. Such terms cannot be found in the writings of Peter or John. If we could tell Peter that the church is the Body of Christ, he might reply, "Where did you hear this? I was close to the Lord Jesus for three and a half years, but I never heard such a word. I heard about the cross and about feeding the Lord's lambs. In my first Epistle I even charged the elders to shepherd the flock of God. But I have never heard about the Body of Christ." We must admit that concerning the matter of the Head and the Body, Paul's vision was higher than Peter's. Although John tells us that Christ is the vine and that we are the branches, he does not say that Christ is the Head and that we are the Body. This is a further indication that without Paul's gospel the revelation in the New Testament would not be complete.

When Christianity went to China hundreds of years ago, all that was made available to the Chinese was a rather poor translation of the four Gospels. The unfortunate Chinese could hear only those aspects of the gospel found in Matthew, Mark, Luke, and John. Although they may have gained some understanding of the forgiveness of sins, I doubt that they had a proper understanding of the kingdom of heaven in Matthew or of eternal life in John. Certainly they had no opportunity to hear the gospel which declares that the believers have Christ in them as their hope of glory and that they are members of the Body of Christ. They could not know that Christ is the Head of the Body of which we are members. What a loss it would be not to have the gospel of Paul!

It is crucial for us to see that Paul's ministry was a completing ministry, a ministry of completing the divine revelation. Paul's gospel is the gospel of completion. Therefore, if we did not have Paul's writings, we would lack a vital part of God's revelation. Paul's Epistles not only complete the divine revelation; they form the very heart of God's revelation in the New Testament. Thus, Paul's gospel is not only the gospel of completion; it is also the center of the New Testament revelation. For this reason, Paul's gospel is the basic gospel.

We in the Lord's recovery need to have a clear view of the gospel according to Paul. The focal point of Paul's gospel is that the Son of God, God's anointed One, has entered into our being to be our life today and our glory in the future so that we may be the members of His Body. This Body, the fullness of the One who fills all in all, is the new man, the household of God, the household of faith, and the true Israel of God. In Paul's gospel there are many mysterious matters that are not covered by Matthew, Mark, Luke, or John. In the four Gospels we are not told that Christ is the mystery of God (Col. 2:2) or that all the fullness of the Godhead dwells in Him bodily (Col. 2:9). In fact, the four Gospels do not even give us a clear word concerning justification by faith. It is in Romans and Galatians that justification by faith is covered in a clear way.

There is no doubt that Matthew speaks clearly and emphatically about the kingdom, which is a matter of administration. However, according to the revelation given to Paul, the gospel is not centered on God's administration. It is focused on the Triune God being our life in order to be

one with us and to make us one with Him, that we may be
the Body of Christ to express God in a corporate way. The
focal point of the gospel is not God's administration; it is
God Himself in His Trinity becoming the processed all-
inclusive Spirit to be life and everything to us for our enjoyment, so that He and we may be one to express Him for
eternity. Such a profound thought cannot be found in the
four Gospels. I doubt that Mark was clear about such a
revelation of God's economy when he was writing his
Gospel.

Many Christians today are not clear about this matter
either. They may be familiar with the councils, the creeds,
and the teachings of the historic church, but they do not
know Paul's revelation of the Triune God processed to
become the all-inclusive Spirit. This indicates that few
Christians adequately know the gospel according to Paul.

Important aspects of Paul's gospel are found in Galatians. We have seen that in 1:15 and 16 Paul says that it
pleased God to reveal His Son in him. What a wonderful
word! However, millions of Christians have no realization
that Christ is in them. In 2:20 Paul goes on to speak of
Christ living in us, and in 4:19, of Christ being formed in
us. In chapter six he covers fourteen important items: the
human spirit (vv. 1, 18), the law of Christ (the law of life,
v. 2), the Spirit (v. 8), eternal life (v. 8), the household
(v. 10), the faith (v. 10), the cross of Christ (v. 14), the religious world, which has been crucified to Paul and to which
Paul has been crucified (v. 14), the new creation (v. 15),
peace (v. 16), mercy (v. 16), the Israel of God (v. 16), the
brands of Jesus (v. 17), and the grace of Christ (v. 18). A
number of these items can be found only in the writings of
Paul, not in any of the four Gospels.

However, we by no means depreciate the four Gospels.
We have devoted much time to the study of Matthew and
John in particular. My purpose here is to emphasize our
need to know the fifth gospel, the gospel of Paul. Some
Christians boast that they accept all ministries, but ac-
tually they do not wholly accept the ministry of Paul. This

indicates that they receive the four Gospels, but do not fully receive the fifth.

The traditional understanding of the gospel in Christianity is very narrow. It does not include the whole gospel revealed in the New Testament. When I was young, my view of the gospel was limited. I only saw that Jesus loved us and died for us so that our sins could be forgiven. I knew nothing of the marvelous aspects of the gospel unfolded in the Epistles of Paul. Even some of today's pastors do not adequately know Paul's gospel revealed in the one hundred chapters of his Epistles.

I. THE GOSPEL OF GRACE

Paul's gospel is the gospel of grace (1:6). Grace is the Triune God, the Father, Son, and Spirit, processed to become our enjoyment. According to 1:6, we have been called in the grace of Christ. Through Christ we enjoy the processed all-inclusive Triune God. The gospel of grace is versus the law of Moses. John 1:17 says, "For the law was given through Moses; grace and reality came through Jesus Christ." In John 1:16 we are told that "of His fullness we all received, and grace upon grace." To receive grace upon grace is to continually receive of the processed Triune God for our enjoyment.

II. THE UNIQUE GOSPEL

The gospel preached by the Apostle Paul was the unique gospel. It was the gospel of Christ (Gal. 1:7). Those who preach a so-called gospel that is different from the unique gospel pervert and distort the gospel of Christ and should be accursed (1:7-9).

III. NOT ACCORDING TO MAN

In 1:11 Paul says, "For I make known to you, brothers, concerning the gospel preached by me, that it is not according to man." Paul received a marvelous revelation of the gospel directly from the Lord Himself. Therefore, the gospel he preached was not according to man.

IV. NOT RECEIVED FROM MAN

In verse 12 Paul goes on to say, "For neither did I receive it from man." Concerning the gospel, Paul did not receive anything from Peter, John, or James.

V. NOT TAUGHT BY MAN

In verse 12 Paul also says that he was not taught the gospel by man. Again and again he emphasizes the fact that man was not the source of his gospel. He did not receive the gospel from man's teaching.

VI. RECEIVED THROUGH THE REVELATION
OF JESUS CHRIST

Paul concludes verse 12 with the words, "I received it through a revelation of Jesus Christ." This refers to the revelation given to the Apostle Paul by the Lord Jesus Christ concerning the gospel. We do not know in what way the gospel was revealed to Paul. Perhaps Paul received this revelation during his stay in Arabia.

Paul's writings testify to the fact that he had received revelation directly from Christ. In his Epistles there are many marvelous expressions which no man could utter apart from divine revelation. Certain ancient philosophers, such as Confucius, have composed some writings that are regarded as important. But there is no comparison between the best of these writings and those of the Apostle Paul. As one who is familiar with the works of Confucius, I can testify that comparing his writings to the Epistles of Paul is like comparing clay to gold. If Paul had not received revelation from Christ, how could he have written the things he did? It would have been impossible. His writings prove that his gospel was not according to man, that it was not received from man, and that it was not taught by man, but that it was received through a revelation of Jesus Christ. The expressions Paul uses are too wonderful to have come from any source other than a revelation directly from the Lord Jesus Christ.

VII. PREACHING THIS GOSPEL
AS A SLAVE OF CHRIST

In verse 10 Paul says, "For am I now persuading men or God? Or do I seek to please men? If I were still pleasing men, I would not be a slave of Christ." Paul was not seeking for men's approval; neither was he seeking to appease men or to satisfy them. As a slave of Christ, he preached the gospel according to the revelation he received, not to please men, but to please God.

LIFE-STUDY OF GALATIANS

MESSAGE THREE

GOD'S SON VERSUS MAN'S RELIGION

Scripture Reading: Gal. 1:13-16

In 1:13-16 we see the matter of God's Son versus man's religion. Verses 13 and 14 present a vivid picture of man's religion. In verse 13 Paul says, "For you have heard of my manner of life formerly in Judaism, that I persecuted the church of God excessively and ravaged it." Here we see a contrast between the Jewish religion and the church of God. When Paul was in Judaism, he persecuted the church because the church was different from his religion. Paul hated the church because it detracted from his religion. In his religious zeal, he persecuted the church of God excessively and ravaged it.

In verse 14 Paul goes on to say, "And I advanced in Judaism beyond many contemporaries in my race, being more exceedingly zealous of the traditions of my fathers." The traditions here were those in the sect of the Pharisees, to which Paul belonged. He called himself "a Pharisee, the son of a Pharisee" (Acts 23:6). The Jewish religion was composed not only of the God-given law and its rituals, but also of man-made traditions. Because Paul was so zealous for the traditions of his fathers, he became a leading religionist and advanced beyond many of his contemporaries.

GOD'S PLEASURE TO REVEAL HIS SON IN US

Then in verses 15 and 16 Paul declares, "But when it pleased God . . . to reveal His Son in me. . . ." At the time appointed by God, when Saul, zealous in his religion, was persecuting the church, the Son of God was revealed to him. God could bear with Saul's zeal for the traditions of his fathers, for this produced a dark background against which to reveal Christ. At a time which was pleasing to Him, God revealed His Son in Saul of Tarsus. God was pleased to reveal to him the living Person of the Son of God. To reveal His Son in us is also a pleasure to God. It is Christ, the Son of God, not the law, in whom God the Father is always pleased (Matt. 3:17; 12:18; 17:5).

The Son of God as the embodiment and expression of God the Father (John 1:18; 14:9-11; Heb. 1:3) is life to us (John 10:10; 1 John 5:12; Col. 3:4). The desire of God's heart is to reveal His Son in us that we may know Him, receive Him as our life (John 17:3; 3:16), and become the sons of God (John 1:12; Gal. 4:5-6). As the Son of the living God (Matt. 16:16), Christ is far superior to Judaism and its traditions (Gal. 1:13-14). The Judaizers bewitched the Galatians so that they considered the ordinances of the law above the Son of the living God. Hence, the apostle in the opening of this Epistle testified that he had been deeply involved in that realm and far advanced in it. God, however, had rescued him out of that course of the world, which was evil in God's eyes, by revealing His Son in him. In his experience, Paul realized that there is no comparison between the Son of the living God and Judaism with its dead traditions from his fathers.

In 1:16 Paul emphasizes the fact that the Son of God was revealed in him. This indicates that God's revealing of His Son to us is in us, not outwardly but inwardly; not by an outward vision but by an inward seeing. This is not an objective revelation; it is a subjective one.

God made the Apostle Paul a minister of Christ by setting him apart, calling him, and revealing His Son in him. Therefore, what Paul preached was not the law, but Christ the Son of God. Furthermore, he did not merely preach the doctrine concerning Christ; he preached Christ as a living Person.

THE LIVING PERSON OF THE SON OF GOD

The crucial point in this message is that this living Person, God's Son, is versus man's religion. This was true at the time of Saul of Tarsus, it has been true throughout the centuries, and it is true today. Instead of focusing his attention on this living Person, man has a natural tendency to direct his attention to religion with its tradition. But from Genesis 1 through Revelation 22 the Bible reveals a living Person. God cares only for this living Person, not for anything else.

The record of the experience of the disciples with the Lord Jesus on the mount of transfiguration illustrates this (Matt. 17:1-8). After bringing Peter, James, and John up into a high mountain apart, the Lord Jesus "was transfigured before them, and His face shone as the sun, and His garments became white as the light" (Matt. 17:2). Along with the other two disciples, Peter saw the Lord's glory. He also saw Moses and Elijah speaking with Him. Although it is doubtful that Moses and Elijah were in glory, they nonetheless were speaking with the glorified Jesus. According to Matthew 17:4, Peter said to Jesus, "Lord, it is good for us to be here; if You are willing, I will make three tabernacles here, one for You, and one for Moses, and one for Elijah." In making this suggestion, Peter was elevating Moses and Elijah to the same level as that of the Lord Jesus. He was heir of the centuries-old tradition concerning Moses, who represented the law, and Elijah, who represented the prophets. To the Jews, Moses and Elijah were the representatives of the entire Old Testament. Hence, even on the mount of transfiguration, Peter was zealous for the traditions regarding Moses and Elijah. But while Peter was still speaking, "behold, a bright cloud overshadowed them, and behold, a voice out of the cloud, saying, This is My beloved Son, in Whom I delight; hear Him!" (Matt. 17:5). Moses and Elijah then disappeared from the scene. When the disciples lifted up their eyes, "they saw no one except Jesus Himself alone." This indicates that in the eyes of God there is no place for religion or tradition — only the living Person of His Son has a place.

TREASURING TRADITIONS IN PLACE OF CHRIST

Man has a natural tendency to appreciate traditional things. How people treasure their traditions! For example, the Seventh-Day Adventists treasure the Sabbath day. They fondly cling to the tradition of the seventh-day Sabbath. But according to Colossians 2:16, the Sabbath is a shadow of which the reality, the body, is Christ. Now that Christ has come, we should turn from the shadow to the reality. Nevertheless, like the Jews of old, today's Seventh-Day Adventists treasure the shadow and neglect Christ. Christ is our day. He is not only our real Sabbath, but the reality of every day. How foolish to treasure the seventh-day Sabbath when we can enjoy Christ as our real Sabbath and as the reality of every day!

Some Christians treasure certain things that are far more ridiculous than this. Have you heard that some preachers are occupied with the lengthening of legs? Where is Christ in such a practice? Those who specialize in the lengthening of legs should call themselves "leg-lengtheners," not ministers of Christ. To associate the lengthening of legs with the name of Christ is to use His name in vain.

Today millions of Christians are occupied with miracles, healing, prophecy, speaking in tongues, the so-called manifestation of gifts, and head covering, but few are occupied with Christ. What a pitiful situation!

For seven and a half years, I was with a very strict Brethren assembly. During my time with them, I heard a good number of messages on the books of Daniel and Revelation. In these messages a great deal was said about beasts, horns, toes, and certain periods of days. As a young man zealous for knowledge, I was somewhat satisfied by that kind of teaching. But although I heard many messages about different aspects of prophecy, I did not hear very

much concerning Christ. Actually the book of Revelation is not focused on beasts, toes, and horns; it is focused
on Christ. This book is a revelation of the Person of Christ.
Even the book of Daniel reveals Christ. Nevertheless, the
messages given in that Brethren assembly were by no
means centered on Christ.

If you attend the so-called Sunday morning services in
today's Christianity or go to Bible studies held by Christian teachers, you will hear about many things. But rarely
will you hear a message in which Christ is unveiled and
ministered to the Lord's people. This indicates that today,
as it has been for centuries, religious people are zealous for
religious things and for traditions, but not for Christ. A
great many Christians care for religion and traditions, but
they do not care for the living Person of Christ.

THE SON, THE FATHER, AND THE SPIRIT

The focal point of the Bible is not practices, doctrines,
or ordinances — it is the living Person of the Son of God. In
1:15 and 16 Paul said that it pleased God to reveal His Son
in him. Concerning the Son of God, many are still under
the influence of the traditional teachings in Christianity
with respect to the Trinity. The New Testament reveals
that God the Father loved the world and gave His Son for
us (John 3:16). But the problem we face is how to understand this. In what way did the Father send His Son? One
day, Philip said to the Lord Jesus, "Lord, show us the
Father and it suffices us" (John 14:8). Surprised at such a
request, the Lord said, "Am I so long a time with you, and
you have not known Me, Philip? He who has seen Me has
seen the Father. How is it that you say, Show us the
Father?" (v. 9). Then the Lord went on to say, "Do you
not believe that I am in the Father, and the Father is in
Me?" (v. 10). However, later on in this chapter, in verse 16,
the Lord Jesus said, "And I will ask the Father, and He will
give you another Comforter, that He may be with you
forever." If I had been Philip, I would immediately have
said, "Lord, since to see You is to see the Father, why do

You now say that You will pray to the Father? Your word seems contradictory." Nevertheless, the Lord Jesus said that He would ask the Father and that the Father would give the disciples another Comforter to be with them forever, even the Spirit of reality (v. 17), who had been abiding with the disciples and who would be in them. But then in verse 18 He says, "I will not leave you orphans; I am coming to you." This indicates that the very He who is the Spirit of reality in verse 17 becomes the I who is the Lord Himself in verse 18. This shows that after His resurrection the Lord would become the Spirit of reality.

My purpose in speaking of these matters from John 14 is to point out that if we are adequately enlightened through the record of the New Testament, we shall see that whenever the Son of God is mentioned, the Father is involved also. We cannot separate the Son from the Father or from the Spirit. Many Christians mistakenly separate the Son from the Father and the Spirit from the Son, claiming that They are three separate and distinct Persons. But such a separation is not according to God's revelation in the New Testament. The Bible reveals that where the Son is, there the Father is, and there the Spirit is also. The Father is embodied in the Son, and the Son is realized as the Spirit. This means that the Spirit is the realization of the Son, who is the embodiment of the Father. For this reason, in 2 Corinthians 13:14 Paul says, "The grace of the Lord Jesus Christ, and the love of God, and the fellowship of the Holy Spirit be with you all" (Gk.). We cannot have the grace of Christ the Son without the love of God the Father or the fellowship of the Holy Spirit. The grace of the Son, the love of the Father, and the fellowship of the Spirit cannot be separated. Actually, these three things are one. In the same principle, we cannot separate the Spirit from the Son nor the Son from the Father. The Father, the Son, and the Spirit all are one. Otherwise, God would not be triune. The word triune is composed of tri-, meaning three, and -une, meaning one. As the Triune God, God is both three in one and one in three.

THE EMBODIMENT OF THE TRIUNE GOD
REALIZED AS THE ALL-INCLUSIVE SPIRIT

It is significant that in Galatians 1:15 and 16 Paul does not say that God revealed Christ in him, but that He revealed His Son in him. Speaking of Christ does not lead to the same kind of involvement as does speaking of the Son. The reason for this difference is that whenever we speak of the Son of God, we are immediately involved with the Father and the Spirit. According to the writings of Paul, to have the Son is to have both the Father and the Spirit. As we have pointed out repeatedly, the Son is the embodiment of the Triune God realized as the Spirit for our enjoyment. Hence, when Paul says that it pleased God to reveal His Son in him, this means that the One revealed in him was the embodiment of the Triune God realized as the processed all-inclusive Spirit. The burden I have received from the Lord is to minister this matter to God's chosen people. Although I have been ministering on this for many years, I can testify that this burden is heavier today than ever before.

In Paul's Epistles we see that the Son is the mystery of God, the embodiment of God, and the One in whom the fullness of the Godhead dwells bodily (Col. 2:2, 9). One day, through incarnation, the Son of God became a man called the last Adam, who, through death and resurrection, has become the life-giving Spirit (1 Cor. 15:45). In 2 Corinthians 3:17 Paul says, "Now the Lord is the Spirit." Putting all these verses together, we see that the Son of God, the embodiment of the fullness of the Godhead, became a man and that in resurrection this One is now the life-giving Spirit.

Concerning Christ as the Son of God, there are two "becomes." According to John 1:14, the Word, the Son of God, became flesh; that is, He became a man. Furthermore, according to 1 Corinthians 15:45, this One, called the last Adam, has become the life-giving Spirit. This is the reason that Paul can say explicitly that now the Lord is the Spirit. The Son of God is thus the embodiment of the Triune God realized as the all-inclusive Spirit. This wonderful Person is versus man's religion.

GOD'S UNIQUE INTENTION

The heart of God is fully occupied with the living Person of His Son. Because His attention is focused on this living Person, God has no interest in giving us things such as immersion, tongues-speaking, healing, circumcision, the Sabbath, head covering, or doctrines about prophecy. God's unique intention is to give us His Son as a living Person.

However, because of the fall, we are easily distracted to care for other things in place of Christ. It is quite possible that even among us in the Lord's recovery we may care for any number of things instead of Christ. For instance, we may care more about the church service than we care for Christ. It is crucial for us to have a vision of this all-inclusive living Person. This Person includes the Father, the Son, and the Spirit; He includes divinity and humanity. Although this living Person is so all-inclusive, He is very practical to us, for, as the life-giving Spirit, He is in our regenerated spirit. On the one hand, He is in the heavens as the Lord, the Christ, the King, the Head, the High Priest, and the heavenly Minister; on the other hand, He is in our spirit to be everything to us. He is God, the Father, the Redeemer, the Savior, man, life, light, and the reality of every positive thing. This is the living Person of the Son of God.

THE LIVING PERSON REVEALED

We have pointed out that Paul's Epistles were written according to God's revelation. But we also need to see that a very high degree of intelligence was required to interpret this revelation and to express it in words. Others may receive such a revelation, but, unlike Paul, they may not have the ability to understand it and to convey it in language. We have seen that Paul, a highly educated person, was a leading religionist. According to his darkened mentality, nothing could compare to Judaism with its law, Scriptures, priestly service, and traditions. As one who always pursued what he thought was best, he was wholly given to these things. He despised the followers of Jesus; he considered that they were merely following an insignificant Nazarene, whereas he was zealous for the traditions of his fathers. But one day, when it pleased God the Father, the living Person of the Son of God was revealed in him. When this Person appeared to him, he fell to the ground and spontaneously called, "Who art thou, Lord?" (Acts 9:5). Immediately the Lord replied, "I am Jesus whom thou persecutest." According to the darkened understanding of Saul of Tarsus, Jesus had been buried in a tomb, and His disciples had stolen His body and hidden it somewhere. But now Saul was shocked to realize that Jesus was living, was speaking from the heavens, and was being revealed to him. From the time this living Person was revealed in Saul, the veil was taken away and Saul's keen mind was enlightened with respect to the Son of God. Henceforth, he cared for this Person and no longer cared for religion or tradition.

Pray that you may see such a vision of the living Person of the Son of God. Also pray that others will see this vision. Pray that they will see this living Person and care for Him instead of things such as the Sabbath, head covering, healing, and spiritual gifts. We need to pray that we shall care for this living Person more than anything, even more than for the church life. Without this living Person as the reality and content of the church life, even the church life will become a tradition. Oh, it is vital that we see this living Person!

THE LIVING PERSON VERSUS ALL THINGS

Though we have a good deal of knowledge of Bible doctrine, our burden is not to minister doctrine; it is to minister the living Son of God as the embodiment of the processed Triune God realized as the life-giving Spirit. We should not treasure anything, including our Bible knowledge or spiritual experience and attainments, in place of this living Person. Daily and hourly, we need to experience this living Person. The church is the Body of this Person, His practical and living expression.

Because this living Person is everything to us, there is no need for us to seek mere holiness, spirituality, victory, love, or submission. As the embodiment of the Triune God realized as the all-inclusive life-giving Spirit, He is within us to be whatever we need. In a forthcoming message we shall see that this One is now living in us. What we lack is not holiness or victory — it is this living Person. He is versus everything. Without Him, everything is a tradition made either by others or by ourselves. May we all see that today this living Person is versus all things.

Apart from Christ, the living Person of the Son of God, whatever we have is religion. For example, a brother may love his wife. But if he loves her apart from Christ, even this is religious. The same is true of sisters who submit to their husbands apart from Christ. This kind of submission is religious and traditional. I have known some Chinese wives who were submissive simply because they were submissive by nature. Before they were saved, they were submissive. After they became Christians, they became good, submissive, Christian wives. But this kind of submission has nothing to do with Christ. It is the expression of Chinese tradition, not of the living Person of the Son of God.

I am concerned that many of us are trying to practice the church life apart from Christ. If this is the case, our church life will be nothing more than a religion with its own kind of tradition. How desperately we need a vision of this living Person! It is crucial that He be revealed in us.

Before I received a vision of the living Person, I was one who kept many traditions. But one day it pleased God to reveal His Son in me. Now I know that this living Person is the embodiment of the processed, all-inclusive Triune God realized in my spirit as the life-giving Spirit. In my spirit I enjoy Him, experience Him, partake of His riches, and live Him. To be a Christian is to be one who is occupied with the living Person, not with religion. Judaism is a religion formed by man in dead letters with vain traditions. But the Son of God is life, the uncreated, eternal life of God. For our experience and enjoyment, this One is the all-inclusive Spirit with the divine reality (John 1:14; 14:6). I do not want anything to do with religion — I want this living Person. Which do you choose — man's religion or the living Person of God's Son?

LIFE-STUDY OF GALATIANS

THE REVELATION OF GOD'S SON IN US

Scripture Reading: Gal. 1:15a, 16a; 2 Cor. 3:14-17; 4:3-6

As a living Person, Christ is spiritual and mysterious. Apart from God's revelation of His Son in us, no human being would be able to see this living Person. Due to the shortage of revelation, millions of people have not realized anything of this Person, even though He is living, real, active, and aggressive. Hence, the problem today is the lack of revelation.

Christians may read the Bible and study it carefully, but see very little of Christ. This also may be our situation even in the Lord's recovery. From the beginning of the Bible to the end, especially in the New Testament, Christ occupies the central place. God's revelation throughout the Scriptures is altogether focused on Christ. Nevertheless, as we review our past experience, we shall have to admit that in our reading of the Bible we did not see much of Christ.

For seven and a half years, I sat under some teachers among the Brethren. Although I heard many messages and took note of the important points, I saw virtually nothing as far as Christ is concerned. I saw a vivid picture of the great image in Daniel 2, a picture I can easily recall today. However, during my years with the Brethren, I did not see Christ.

VEILS KEEPING US FROM KNOWING CHRIST

Concerning the revelation of God's Son in us, Paul covers two cases in 2 Corinthians 3 and 4, the case of the Jews in particular and the case of the unbelievers in general. When the Jews read the Old Testament, they read

it with their understanding veiled. In 2 Corinthians 3:15
Paul says, "But even unto this day, when Moses is read,
the veil is upon their heart." Do you know what this veil is?
It is the religion of Judaism. If you contact orthodox Jews
today and speak to them about Christ, you will realize that
they are covered with a thick, strong veil. The same is true
of Moslems and even of many Christians. For example,
many of those in the Catholic Church who truly believe in
Christ are covered with a veil of many layers, perhaps
dozens of layers. One of these veils concerns the superstition that Mary is the mother of God. These believers
persist in saying that they must continue to pray to Mary,
the so-called mother of God, because they think their experience proves that prayers to the so-called holy mother are
heard and answered. What a veil this is!

Seventh-Day Adventists are veiled by their observance
of the seventh-day Sabbath. As you speak to them
concerning Christ, you will find what a thick veil this ordinance is to them.

As you contact Christians today, you will find that virtually all Christians are veiled in some way. These veils
keep them from seeing Christ.

Although Christ is spiritual and mysterious, God has
created within us an organ by which we can know Christ.
This organ is the human spirit. In his subtlety, Satan has
blinded people to the fact that they have a spirit, or has
otherwise kept them from using their spirit. Instead, he en-
tices them to use their fallen mentality, which is blinded,
darkened, and hardened. In 2 Corinthians 3:14 Paul says
that the Jewish religionists are hardened in their thoughts
(Gk.). To be hardened in this way is also to be blind and in
darkness. Many Christians also are blinded, hardened, and
darkened because they are covered with so many veils.
These veils not only frustrate them from knowing Christ,
but often keep them from recognizing the church people as
genuine Christians. Some persist in considering us as a
cult.

Furthermore, the veils that cover today's Christians

make them very touchy. If they are touched even slightly, they are offended. The reason for this touchiness is that Satan, the subtle one, the touchy one, is crouching in their minds. Satan is lurking in the mentality of today's veiled Christians. What a pitiful situation that so many genuine believers in Christ are still veiled!

We need to apply this word about veils to ourselves. It is crucial that we be on the alert, for it is possible for anything that is not Christ Himself to be used as a veil by the subtle one. Satan may use even the Scriptures or the law given by God as veils. In Romans 7 Paul says that the law is good, holy, and spiritual. But even such a good, holy, and spiritual thing in the hands of Satan can become a veil. This indicates that Satan can use even the highest spiritual gift to veil our understanding. Thus, it is possible for anything that is not Christ Himself to be a veil.

UNBELIEVERS BLINDED
BY THE GOD OF THIS AGE

In 2 Corinthians 4, Paul gives us the general case. In verse 4 he says that the god of this age has blinded the thoughts of those who do not believe (Gk.). The god of this age is Satan. Those who are blinded or veiled think that they do not worship anything. Actually, their god is Satan. Atheists worship Satan without knowing what they are doing. All people today, whether primitive or highly cultured, have been blinded by the god of this age. Consider all those you see on the street or in the supermarkets. How few of them know God! This is true even among a vast number of those who go to today's chapels, cathedrals, and denominational buildings. There is little revelation of the Son of God, and there is veil upon veil to keep people from knowing Christ. In their blindness, many condemn those who have seen the vision of the living Person of the Son of God.

THE NEED TO DROP OUR CONCEPTS

If we would receive the revelation of the Son of God,

we need to drop our concepts. Every concept, whether
spiritual or carnal, is a veil. I have spent many years grop-
ing in my search to learn how to have revelation. Eventually I discovered that to have revelation we need to drop
our concepts.

God today is shining everywhere. This age of grace is an
age of light. God is shining, and the Bible is shining also.
The Bible is full of light, and it has been printed in
hundreds of languages. Moreover, the all-inclusive Spirit
moving on earth is full of grace. But although the Bible is
shining and the Spirit is moving, many still do not receive
revelation. The reason is that they hold to certain concepts
and are veiled by these concepts. As you contact people
from various nationalities, you will find that all of them are
strong in their concepts. This is also true among us in the
Lord's recovery. On the one hand, I worship the Lord for all
the growth and improvement among us. On the other
hand, I realize that many veils still remain. These veils are
the concepts that blind us.

With respect to receiving revelation, there is no
problem on God's side. On His side everything is ready.
The problem is altogether on our side. We need to drop the
veils, that is, to drop our concepts. It is important for us to
pray, "Lord, help me to drop everything that is a veil." If
you hold on to your concepts while reading the Bible, you
will be like the ancient Jews who had a veil on their mind
whenever the Scriptures were read. But if you drop your
concepts as your read the Word, you will read it with an
unveiled face. Then the light will shine into you subjectively.

I was born into Christianity, and from childhood I
heard about Christ. However, I was not saved until I was
nineteen years old. I knew about Jesus, and I was in favor
of Christianity. But I was not saved until the Son of God
was revealed in me. One day, when I was nineteen, God
shined into me, and I received a revelation of the Lord
Jesus. At that time I began to have direct personal contact
with Him and to know Him as a living Person. I touched

Him, and I was touched by Him. Between Him and me there was a living transaction, a living contact. We all need a direct, personal, living contact with the living Person of the Son of God.

TURNING OUR HEARTS TO THE LORD

Today many of us earnestly desire to live Christ. But to live Christ we need revelation. As we have pointed out again and again, the only way revelation can come to us is if we drop our concepts. We also need to pray, "Lord, I trust in You to defeat the god of this age. Apart from You, I do not worship anything. Lord, I turn my heart to You, and I drop all my concepts. I don't want to worship anyone other than You." If you pray in this way, the light will shine, and you will receive revelation. If you drop your concepts and turn your heart to the Lord, the veils will be taken away, and the god of this age will have no ground in your being.

The light is here, and it is shining. Our problem is that our heart is turned away to many other things, and therefore we are covered with layer upon layer of veils. This enables the god of this age to have ground in us. As a result, our thoughts are darkened, blinded, and hardened, and we cannot receive revelation, even though we may read the Bible and listen to messages. Oh, how we need revelation!

The Lord was very merciful to Saul of Tarsus. First, He knocked him down and then caused him to drop all the veils. Before the Lord appeared to him on the way to Damascus, Saul was altogether veiled. According to his opinion, Jesus the Nazarene had been terminated. He had been crucified and buried, and was in the tomb. But when Saul was on the way to Damascus, the Lord Jesus appeared to him from the heavens, and spontaneously Saul called, "Who art thou, Lord?" The Lord Jesus replied, "I am Jesus whom thou persecutest." The Lord's answer took away a thick veil. The light of the gospel of the glory of Christ shined into Saul of Tarsus, and he saw the glory of God in the face of Christ.

If we would see such a revelation of the living Person, we must begin by dropping our veils, our concepts. Second, we need to turn our hearts to the Lord. According to 2 Corinthians 3:16, when the heart turns to the Lord, the veil will be taken away. The more you turn your heart to the Lord, the less ground the god of this age will have in your life and in your being. Then you will be under the shining of the heavenly light, and you will receive the revelation of the living Person.

I can testify that in the early years of my Christian life, I had little revelation. I was veiled. But one day the veils began to drop, and the light shined into me. Since that time, the light has been coming again and again. For this reason, it is not difficult for me to receive revelation. Let us all drop the veils and, by His mercy and grace, turn our hearts to Him.

GOD'S PLEASURE

In 1:15 and 16 Paul says that it pleased God to reveal His Son in him. This indicates that to reveal the Son of God brings pleasure to God. Nothing is more pleasing to God than the unveiling, the revelation, of the living Person of the Son of God.

AN INWARD REVELATION

Furthermore, this revelation is an inward revelation. Although I have never seen the Lord Jesus outwardly in a physical way, I have seen Him inwardly. I have received an inward revelation of this living Person. This inward revelation is in our spirit through our enlightened mind. Because the mind plays an important part, it is crucial that we drop our concepts, all of which are in the mind. If we hold on to concepts in our mind, the revelation may be in our spirit, but it will not be able to penetrate our veiled mentality. We need to drop our concepts so that our mind may be released and become transparent. Then when the Spirit shines in our spirit, this shining will come into our

transparent mind. Then we shall receive an inward
revelation.

A SUBJECTIVE REVELATION

This inward revelation of Christ is subjective. It is not
objective like the so-called visions in the Pentecostal move-
ment. I have been in meetings where people claimed to see
a bright light in a certain corner of the room. The revelation about which we are speaking in this message is
nothing of such an outward nature. Rather, it is altogether
subjective.

IN OUR SPIRIT BY THE SPIRIT

This subjective revelation is given in our spirit by the
Spirit (Eph. 1:17; 3:5). Our spirit and the Spirit of God
both are realities. We cannot deny that within us we have a
human spirit. Neither can we deny that the divine Spirit is
in our spirit. In order to receive the revelation of the Son of
God, we must first drop our concepts. Second, we must
turn our hearts to the Lord and worship nothing other than
Him. Third, we must take care of the depths of our being,
that is, of our spirit. It is in our spirit that the Spirit is shining, revealing Christ in us and speaking to us concerning
Christ. It is also helpful to pray-read the Word, especially
verses from the Epistles of Paul. This will enable us to see
Christ and to receive a subjective revelation of this living
Person.

The subjective revelation about which we are speaking
here is concerned only with the living Person of the Son of
God. For the sake of receiving such a revelation, may we all
learn to drop our concepts, to turn our heart to the Lord, to
pay attention to our spirit, and to pray over verses from the
writings of Paul. Then the Spirit will enlighten us and
speak to us of Christ. As a result, we shall receive a subjective revelation of the Son of God.

MAKING US A NEW CREATION

The more revelation we receive of the Son of God, the

more He will live in us. The more He lives in us, the more He will become to us the unique and central blessing of the gospel which God promised to Abraham. This means that He will be to us the all-inclusive land realized as the all-inclusive, processed, life-giving Spirit. This should not simply be a doctrine to us. If we drop our concepts, turn our heart to the Lord, pay attention to the spirit, and spend time in the Word, Christ will be revealed in us, He will live in us, and He will be formed in us. Day by day, He will become more of an enjoyment to us. As a result, this living Person will make us a new creation in a practical way. The book of Galatians eventually brings us to the new creation by way of the inward revelation of the living Person of the Son of God.

Let us daily practice receiving revelation by dropping our concepts and turning our hearts to the Lord. The way to receive an inward, subjective, spiritual revelation is always to drop our concepts, to turn our heart to the Lord, and to tell the Lord that we hold on to nothing besides Him and that our heart is wholly for Him. Then if we pay attention to our spirit and spend time in the Word, we shall receive revelation. The living Person will live in us and be formed in us. We shall enjoy Him more and more, and He will make us a new creation.

Paul's burden in writing the book of Galatians, and our need today, is that we be brought into a state where we are full of the revelation of the Son of God and thereby become a new creation with Christ living in us, being formed in us, and being enjoyed by us continually as the all-inclusive Spirit.

LIFE-STUDY OF GALATIANS

THE FORMATION OF PAUL'S APOSTLESHIP

Scripture Reading: Gal. 1:15-24

In 1:15-24 we see the formation of Paul's apostleship. As we consider these verses, we need to see not only how Paul's apostleship was formed, but also how we can be formed into today's apostles, God's present-day sent ones. In the Life-study of Ephesians we pointed out that all the believers in Christ can be apostles, those sent by the Lord to fulfill His purpose and to carry out His plan.

We should not hold the concept that we cannot be an apostle like Paul. The apostles are examples of what all believers should be. Paul was not an extraordinary person, and he did not reach a state that no one else can attain. The concept that the apostles are unique is a Roman Catholic tradition. This tradition is related to the concept that Peter was the unique successor of Christ and therefore the first pope. What a devilish concept! Far from being unique, Peter is an example of one who followed the Lord. In particular, he is an example to Jewish believers in Christ. Paul is a pattern especially for Gentile believers. In 1 Timothy 1:16 he says, "Howbeit for this cause I obtained mercy, that in me first Jesus Christ might show forth all long-suffering, for a pattern to them which should hereafter believe on him to life everlasting." Since Paul is our pattern, none of us should say that we cannot be like him.

Although the brothers may believe that they can be today's apostles, the sisters may find it very difficult to believe that this also applies to them. As a help to the sisters, we need to point out that in God's household there are no daughters. God has only sons, not daughters. Christ, the firstborn Son of God, has brothers, but He does not have sisters. This indicates that, according to life, all the believers, including the sisters, are sons of God and brothers of Christ. For this reason, in his Epistles Paul addresses the brothers, but not the brothers and sisters. The sisters, of course, are included in the term brothers.

According to life, all the believers are males. However, according to love, we all are females. Christ is our Bridegroom, and we are His Bride. The relationship between the Bride and the Bridegroom is a matter of love, not a matter of life. Love is the unique requirement of married life. Therefore, we are living sons of the living God, whereas we are the loving Bride of our dear Bridegroom. How, then, would you answer this question: Are we, the believers in Christ, males or females? The proper way to answer is to reply that according to life we are males, but according to love we are females.

Paul was made an apostle not according to love, but according to life. It was as a matter of life that he was made a pattern for all the believers, the brothers and the sisters as well. This indicates that by taking Paul as our pattern, we all, brothers and sisters, can be God's sent ones today. Paul's status was that of an apostle, and ours should be the same. Hence, as we study the formation of Paul's apostleship, we are also studying the formation of our own apostleship.

All of us in the Lord's recovery need to be sent ones. At the least, a young sister can be sent by the Lord to her parents to testify to them about the Lord Jesus. Are you ready to be sent by the Lord? We all should be prepared to be sent forth by Him. Concerning this matter of apostleship, our minds need to be renewed. Therefore, as we consider the various points in this message, we need to see how we can follow Paul's pattern and be formed into apostles. All the points we shall cover are prerequisites for the formation of our apostleship.

I. SET APART BY GOD FROM HIS MOTHER'S WOMB

In 1:15 Paul says that God set him apart from his mother's womb. The Greek indicates being designated or

distinguished for a specific purpose. This setting apart
took place before Paul was born.

When we read about Paul being set apart from his
mother's womb, we may have the concept that this was
true of him, but not of us. This was my point of view when I
read these verses years ago. According to my concept, Paul
had been set apart, but I had not. This concept, however, is
wrong. We were chosen, selected, before the foundation of
the world (Eph. 1:4). Surely to be chosen from before the
foundation of the world is more crucial than to be set apart
from our mother's womb. Since you have been chosen from
before the foundation of the world, do you not believe that
you were also set apart from your mother's womb? Certainly you were. As we shall see, this refers to the carrying
out in time of God's eternal selection.

Some teachers of the Bible have different opinions
concerning the time that Paul was separated from his
mother's womb. According to one school of thought, he was
set apart from the time he was conceived. But according to
another school, he was set apart at the time of birth. There
is no need for us to split hairs concerning this. The main
point here is that according to His selection we were chosen
by God in eternity, before the foundation of the world. This
means that we were chosen before the beginning of time,
in eternity. However, there was the need for us, at a definite time, to be separated from our mother's womb. To
be set apart from our mother's womb is related to the
accomplishment in time of the selection God made in
eternity. It was necessary for us to be born at a certain
time. We thank the Lord that Saul of Tarsus was not born
a hundred years before the Lord Jesus, nor six hundred
years afterward. He was born at just the right time and in
the right place, in the city of Tarsus. It was sovereign of the
Lord that Paul was not born in Galilee, where Peter was
born. Both Peter and Paul were chosen before the foundation of the world, and both were set apart at precisely the
right time. According to God's timing, He caused these two
of His selected ones to be conceived in their mother's
womb. The same is true of us today. We were selected from

before the foundation of the world. Then God waited until
the time was right for us to be born. Hence, regarding our
birth God had His timing. We all were selected in eternity
when Paul was selected; however, we were set apart from
our mother's womb at different times. Therefore, to be set
apart from our mother's womb is to have God's selection
carried out in a practical way.

Do not think that Paul was set apart from his mother's
womb, but that you were not. Because Paul was made a
pattern, what happened to him should happen to us also.
Whenever I recall my past, I worship the Lord. As I consider my youth, I sometimes weep before Him. How I
thank Him that He caused me to be born at just the right
time and in just the right place, more than seventy-four
years ago in a small village in China. We all can say, "Lord,
thank You for setting me apart from my mother's womb." I
hope that we all shall have a full realization of this. We
need to realize that God set us apart in order to carry out
His eternal selection. This was true of Paul, and it is just as
true of us today.

II. CALLED BY GOD THROUGH HIS GRACE

In 1:15 Paul also says that God called him through His
grace. Paul was called to be an apostle through the grace of
Christ, not through the law that came by Moses. This calling took place at the time of his conversion. We also can
testify that we have been called by God. Actually, God's
calling of us began with His setting us apart from our
mother's womb. If we spend time to review our past, we
shall see that God's calling of us began with our conception in the womb. God arranged the time and place of our
birth. Then He called us. How grateful I am to the Lord
that He caused me to be conceived in the womb of one who
was in Christianity, although she was not saved at that
time. In this way God caused me to be born into
Christianity, beginning His calling of me by setting me
apart from my mother's womb. Then one day, in 1925,
God's calling was accomplished in a full way when I
believed in the Lord Jesus. None of us should have any

doubt about being called by God. Rather, let us worship Him and thank Him for His calling. Everything related to us, such as our family and education, is according to God's sovereignty and related to His calling of us.

III. HAVING THE SON OF GOD REVEALED IN HIM

In 1:15 and 16 Paul says that God was pleased to reveal His Son in him. The Son of God was unveiled to Paul and shown to him. This means that he received a vision of the living Person of the Son of God. Since Paul is a pattern of the believers and the Son of God was revealed in him, we also should have Christ revealed in us. When the Son of God is revealed in us, something divine is added to us. Selection and calling do not cause anything to be added into us. But the revelation of the Son of God in us causes divinity to be added to our humanity. God Himself is added into our being to become our life. He who has the Son has life (1 John 5:12). Hence, to have the Son of God revealed in us means to have God added to us to become our life.

IV. NOT CONFERRING WITH FLESH AND BLOOD

After the Son of God was revealed in Paul, he "did not confer with flesh and blood." This means that he did not confer with man, who is made up of flesh and blood. This confirms the fact that Paul did not receive the gospel from man (1:12).

After we believed in the Lord Jesus, many of us immediately conferred with others. If we recall our experience, we shall realize that much of this was of no avail. As soon as I was saved, I turned to various people for help. However, I was only frustrated by them and cooled down. Some of you may have spoken to certain preachers or ministers, only to find that you were discouraged by your contact with them.

When young believers contacted me thirty years ago, I had a great deal to say. But it is much different today. Now when others contact me, I simply tell them to pray and to seek the Lord, to bring everything to Him for His leading. I do not want to be the flesh and blood with which others confer. We should neither confer with flesh and blood, nor should we be the flesh and blood with whom others confer. Let us leave others and their situation to the Lord.

V. NOT GOING UP TO JERUSALEM
TO THOSE WHO WERE APOSTLES BEFORE HIM

Paul opens verse 17 with the words, "Neither did I go up to Jerusalem to those who were apostles before me." We all have made mistakes in this regard. We have gone to a place we consider today's Jerusalem seeking to confer with certain leaders. To go to some Jerusalem to those who were apostles before us is something of tradition and of religion. Actually, it is to confer with flesh and blood.

Some of the leading ones may be concerned that such a word will cause the saints not to seek the proper fellowship. Furthermore, they may think that this will ruin the leadership. But would it not be wonderful for all the saints to be trained not to confer with flesh and blood? How good it would be if we all brought ourselves with our needs and problems directly to the Lord! If we would be today's apostles, we should follow Paul's pattern in not going up to Jerusalem to confer with others.

VI. GOING AWAY TO ARABIA
AWAY FROM OTHER CHRISTIANS
AND RETURNING TO DAMASCUS

In verse 17 Paul says that he "went away to Arabia." It is difficult to trace where in Arabia Paul went and how long he stayed there after his conversion. However, it must have been a place away from other Christians, and the time of his stay there must not have been short. His purpose in saying this was to testify that he did not receive the gospel from man. In Arabia he must have received some revelation concerning the gospel directly from the Lord.

By going to Arabia, Paul went to a place apart from both Jewish culture and Christian influence. According to traditional understanding, Paul stayed in Arabia for three years. Actually, we do not know how long he remained there. We simply know that for a period of time he went apart from Jewish religion and Christian influence. During his stay in Arabia, he probably compared his experience with the Old Testament, which he had come to know so well through the instruction of Gamaliel. I believe that in Arabia Paul had a quiet, sober time of checking his experience with the Old Testament Scriptures. No doubt, he also spent much time in prayer.

Here we see another principle for us to follow. After we have a certain amount of experience directly from the Lord, we need to withdraw from every kind of religious influence to quietly and soberly check our experiences with the Bible. This will be a great help to us. I believe that as Paul was comparing his experience with Scripture, much light and revelation came to him.

In verse 17 Paul also says that he "again returned to Damascus."

VII. AFTER THREE YEARS GOING UP TO JERUSALEM TO SEE CEPHAS AND JAMES

In verses 18 and 19 Paul goes on to say, "Then after three years I went up to Jerusalem to become acquainted with Cephas, and I remained with him fifteen days. But I saw none of the other apostles except James the brother of the Lord." Three years after his return to Damascus, Paul went up to Jerusalem. I believe that during these years he also spent much time in prayer and in checking his experience with the Old Testament.

Although Paul did not confer with flesh and blood, at a certain time he did go up to Jerusalem. To confer with flesh and blood is wrong. However, to isolate ourselves from other members of the Body of Christ is also wrong. After receiving revelation, at the proper time we need to contact those members of the Lord's Body who came to know the Lord ahead of us. There is the need for this kind of fellowship.

VIII. GOING TO SYRIA AND CILICIA
OF THE GENTILE WORLD

In verse 21 Paul continues, "Then I went into the regions of Syria and Cilicia." Arabia, Syria, and Cilicia were all regions of the Gentile world. By mentioning his journeying to all these places, Paul testifies that the revelation he received concerning the gospel was not from any men, any Christians, most of whom at that time were in Judea (v. 22). I believe that in the regions of Syria and Cilicia Paul spent more time praying and considering the Scriptures. Probably he also received further revelation.

IX. UNKNOWN BY FACE TO THE CHURCHES OF JUDEA

Verse 22 says, "Yet I was unknown by face to the churches of Judea which are in Christ." To say this is also to strengthen the point that Paul did not receive the gospel from any who were believers in Christ before him. Hardly any of the saints in Judea had seen him.

X. THE CHURCHES IN JUDEA
HEARING THAT THE FORMER PERSECUTOR
NOW PREACHES THE FAITH WHICH ONCE HE RAVAGED

In verses 23 and 24 Paul concludes, "But they only heard that he who formerly persecuted us now preaches the faith which formerly he ravaged. And they glorified God in me." The churches, including all the believers in Christ in Judea, only heard the news of Paul's conversion and glorified God in him. They had nothing to do with his receiving of the revelation concerning the gospel.

LIFE-STUDY OF GALATIANS

PAUL'S FAITHFULNESS
AND PETER'S UNFAITHFULNESS
TO THE TRUTH OF THE GOSPEL

Scripture Reading: Gal. 2:1-14

In the foregoing messages we have pointed out that Paul was a pattern for the believers, especially for Gentile believers. In particular, the formation of Paul's apostleship is a pattern for the formation of our apostleship today. In this message we come to 2:1-14. In these verses not only do we have a record of how Paul kept the truth; we have a pattern by which we may learn of Paul how we also may keep the truth. Let us firstly consider Paul's faithfulness to the truth of the gospel. Then we shall consider Peter's unfaithfulness.

I. PAUL'S FAITHFULNESS

In Galatians we see that Paul was faithful, honest, frank, and bold. At the same time, he also displayed a spirit of meekness. He refers to such a spirit in 6:1, where he says that those who are spiritual should restore the one overtaken in an offense in a spirit of meekness. In writing this Epistle, Paul was endeavoring to restore the Galatian believers who had been overtaken by their weakness. No doubt, in their subtlety the Judaizers had taken advantage of the weakness of the Galatian believers. Therefore, Paul exercised a spirit of meekness in order to restore the ones who had been overtaken. On the one hand, he was bold; on the other hand, he was meek in spirit. Regarding this, we all need to learn of Paul.

Throughout the years, both in the Far East and in the West, I have learned that much that passes for meekness is actually the playing of politics. Paul certainly was not meek in this way. For example, in 2:4 he speaks of "false brothers, brought in secretly, who stole in to spy out our freedom." In making such a statement, Paul surely was not political. In his choice of terms he was bold and frank.

Those who take the lead in the churches must learn to be honest, faithful, frank, and bold, yet all of this with meekness. We should never play politics. However, if we are short of grace and lack the wisdom to handle a particular situation, we may need to be silent. But we must never be political.

In dealing with the problem in Galatia, Paul faced a situation which was serious and very touchy. In 4:20 he said that he was perplexed about the Galatians. He was puzzled, not knowing how to deal with these distracted believers. But even though Paul was puzzled, he did not play politics. On the contrary, he was still frank, honest, and bold.

Playing politics is a form of lying. In the eyes of God, politics is more evil than an outright lie. This is the reason that the international political situation is so evil, so deplorable, in God's sight. Many diplomats and ambassadors are experts at lying in a subtle way. Some have even been trained to behave in such a manner. The church is altogether another realm, another kingdom. In this realm, the realm of the kingdom of the heavens, there should not be any lying; neither should there be any playing of politics. In John 8:44 the Lord Jesus said that the Devil, Satan, is the father of lies. Since playing politics is even worse than lying, it must also issue from the devilish father of lies. Because the playing of politics is so evil and devilish, negotiations can never bring peace among the nations. How can there be peace among nations when the representatives of those nations lie and play politics? In the church, the earthly embassy of the heavenly kingdom, there should be no playing of politics.

Paul, a good example of a heavenly ambassador, was not political in dealing with the Galatians. He spoke the truth in a frank way. You may feel that Paul was extreme in his frankness. Who else would use such a term as "false brothers"? Would you dare to call someone a false brother? Would you write a letter in which you speak of false brothers who have stolen in to spy out our freedom? Probably none of us would dare to be as frank as Paul was. Furthermore, in 3:1 he addressed the believers as "foolish Galatians." How bold, honest, and genuine Paul was! The Galatian believers certainly were foolish to turn from Christ to the law. They surely were foolish in following the Judaizers. Therefore, Paul addressed them in a bold and frank manner. Let us learn from him to be faithful and bold and not to play politics. If we lack grace or the wisdom, we may be quiet. But if we speak regarding a particular situation, we should not be political.

A. Going Up to Jerusalem according to Revelation

In 2:1 and 2 Paul said, "Then after a period of fourteen years I went up again to Jerusalem with Barnabas, taking Titus with me also. And I went up according to revelation." As recorded in Acts 15, this happened after a number of churches had been raised up in the Gentile world by Paul's preaching (see Acts 13 and 14). This also indicates that Paul's preaching of the gospel to raise up the Gentile churches had nothing to do with the believers in Jerusalem and Judea.

In 1:18 Paul speaks of going up to Jerusalem to become acquainted with Cephas. In 2:1 and 2 we see that after a period of fourteen years, he went up to Jerusalem again, according to revelation. Not only Paul's gospel but also his going up to Jerusalem was according to the Lord's revelation, not according to any organization or system. His moves and activity were according to the Lord's instant leading. This again indicates that his preaching of the gospel was not according to man's teaching, but according to the Lord's direct revelation.

From Paul's experience of going up to Jerusalem after fourteen years according to revelation, we learn that it is

often more difficult not to go to a certain place than it is to
go there. For example, it is easy for me to make the
decision to fly to London. But to refrain from doing so for
fourteen years may not be easy. This requires that I be
restricted. Because Paul was restricted, he did not go to
Jerusalem apart from revelation. However, at a certain
time, according to revelation, he went up to Jerusalem
with Barnabas and Titus.

Paul's visit to Jerusalem refers to the time of Acts 15.
The Judaizers had caused a great deal of trouble by telling
the Gentile believers that they had to be circumcised in
order to be saved. They were making circumcision a condition of God's eternal salvation. This issue was extremely
serious. According to revelation, Paul went up to Jerusalem to deal with the source of the problem. Paul did not
go to Jerusalem to receive revelation or learn some new
teachings. Rather, he went there according to revelation to
deal with the source of a serious problem.

In this matter Paul also is a pattern for us. We should
learn from his example not to go anywhere or to take any
action in a light way. On the contrary, we must be
restricted by the Spirit in our spirit. Whenever we go to a
certain place, we should move according to revelation.

B. Privately Laying the Gospel Which He Preached
before Those of Reputation

In 2:2 Paul also says, "I laid before them the gospel
which I proclaim among the nations, but privately to those
of reputation, lest somehow I should be running or had run
in vain." In doing this, Paul also was restricted. If we were
going up to Jerusalem in that situation, we probably would
have gone up with a great deal of fanfare. Perhaps we
would have sent out advertisements telling people that the
apostle to the Gentile world was coming. This is the way
practiced in today's Christianity. Announcement of the
coming of a well-known preacher or evangelist is made in
advance in order to assure a large crowd. Paul, in contrast

to the way of today's Christianity, presented his gospel privately to certain ones. This indicates that he went up to Jerusalem privately with no intention of speaking before a large congregation. He simply wanted to contact the leading ones, the apostles and elders. This is according to the record of Acts 15, which corresponds to the account in Galatians 2.

C. Not Even Titus Compelled to Be Circumcised

In verse 3 Paul goes on to say, "But not even Titus, who was with me, being a Greek, was compelled to be circumcised." This indicates that Paul in his move for the Lord's testimony did not care for the observance of the law. Paul deliberately refused to have Titus circumcised. Paul's purpose was to keep the truth. Since in Christ circumcision is over, to circumcise a believer would cause the truth to be blurred. Therefore, Paul did not compel Titus to be circumcised.

Judaism was built upon the God-given law with three pillars: circumcision, the Sabbath, and the holy diet. All three were ordained by God (Gen. 17:9-14; Exo. 20:8-11; Lev. 11) as shadows of things to come (Col. 2:16-17). Circumcision was a shadow of the crucifixion of Christ in putting off the flesh as signified in baptism (Col. 2:11). The Sabbath was a type of Christ as the rest for His people (Matt. 11:28-30). The holy diet symbolized the distinction between persons called clean and unclean, those whom God's holy people should contact and those they should not contact (Acts 10:11-16, 34-35). Since Christ has come, all the shadows must be over. Hence, the observance of the Sabbath was abolished by the Lord Jesus in His ministry (Matt. 12:1-12), the holy diet was annulled by the Holy Spirit in Peter's ministry (Acts 10:9-20), and circumcision was counted as nothing in the revelation received by Paul in his ministry (Gal. 5:6; 6:15). Furthermore, the law, the base of Judaism, has been terminated and replaced by Christ (Rom. 10:4; Gal. 2:16). Thus, the entire Judaism is gone.

D. Not Yielding in Subjection to the False Brothers

In verses 4 and 5 Paul continues, "And it was because of the false brothers, brought in secretly, who stole in to spy out our freedom which we have in Christ Jesus that they might bring us into slavery; to whom we yielded in subjection not even for an hour." The false brothers were the Judaizers who perverted the gospel of Christ by smuggling the observances of the law into the church and who troubled the genuine believers in Christ (1:7). The freedom Paul speaks of here is freedom from the bondage of the law. Slavery here refers to slavery under the law.

The false brothers to whom Paul refused to be subject were spreading the concept that believers had to be circumcised in order to be saved. Paul stood against this and did not yield even for an hour. He would not be subject to those who sought to damage our freedom in Christ and to bring us into slavery. To be free in Christ is to enjoy liberation from the bondage of the law with its requirement of circumcision. All the believers are now free from obligation to the law, especially from the obligation to be circumcised. In order to maintain this freedom, Paul refused to have Titus circumcised or to yield in subjection to the Judaizers.

E. Keeping the Truth of the Gospel

Paul refused to yield in subjection to the false brothers so that the truth of the gospel might remain with the believers. All that Paul did, he did on behalf of the believers so that, for their sake, the truth would remain clear.

F. Receiving Nothing from Those of Reputation

In verse 6 Paul says, "But from those who were of reputation as being somewhat (whatever they were, it means nothing to me; God does not accept man's person), for to me those who were of reputation imparted nothing." Here we see that Paul did not receive anything from those of reputation. Peter, John, and James did not have anything to teach Paul. Rather, Paul had much to teach them. More of the New Testament was written by Paul than by anyone else. In his second Epistle, Peter even admitted that in Paul's writings "are some things hard to be understood" (2 Pet. 3:16).

We have pointed out that in Paul's Epistles a number of great items are covered that are not found elsewhere. For example, Paul speaks of the new man, a matter not even hinted at in the Gospels. Furthermore, in his Epistles Paul presents a thorough analysis of our regenerated being. He describes our regenerated spirit, renewed heart, transformed soul, renewed mind, and the condition of our physical body. Neither Peter nor John speaks of these things in such a full way. Consider the picture Paul presents in Romans 8. What a view we have in this chapter of our regenerated being! According to this chapter, to have a regenerated being is to have divinity mingled with our humanity. This means that the element of divinity has been added to our humanity. No other New Testament writer presents this matter in the way Paul does. This indicates that Paul had a great deal to teach other believers. But although Paul knew more and had more, he was not proud.

In Jerusalem there was a lack of the proper atmosphere for Paul to present what he had within him. From a careful reading of Acts 15 we can realize that in Jerusalem there was an atmosphere of superiority. To some extent at least, the apostles there regarded themselves as superior to Paul and Barnabas. Paul and Barnabas were apostles to the uncircumcision, to the Gentiles, whereas those in Jerusalem were apostles to the circumcision. Spiritually speaking, however, Paul was superior to Peter, John, and James. The attitude of superiority that prevailed in Jerusalem was a factor that contributed to the destruction of that city in 70 A.D., about fifteen years after Paul went up to Jerusalem as recorded in Galatians 2.

Paul had seen more than Peter, James, and John had.

They had seen the Lord in the flesh and had come to know
Him according to the flesh. But Paul knew Him in a spiritual way. In 2 Corinthians 5:16 Paul says, "Wherefore
henceforth know we no man after the flesh: yea, though we
have known Christ after the flesh, yet now henceforth know
we him no more." We should seek to know Christ not
according to the flesh, but according to the spirit. Because
Paul knew Christ in spirit, he had seen more and had more
than Peter, John, and James.

This shows us that we should not trust in age or
seniority. Peter, John, and James were older than Paul and
were apostles when he was still a young man persecuting
the followers of the Lord Jesus. But after his conversion,
Paul came to see more of Christ and of God's economy than
anyone else. The book of Romans, for instance, indicates
the depth of Paul's knowledge. Paul certainly had a great
deal to teach those in Jerusalem. But the atmosphere was
not right for him to do so. Therefore, he did not teach them
anything; nevertheless, he did not receive anything from
those of reputation.

G. Having Been Entrusted with
the Gospel of the Uncircumcision

According to verse 7, those in Jerusalem realized that
Paul had been "entrusted with the gospel of the uncircumcision, even as Peter with that of the circumcision." It
was clear that the Lord had entrusted to Paul the gospel of
the uncircumcision. Although concerning this Paul was
frank, honest, faithful, and bold, he was not proud. Rather,
he simply realized that the One who worked in Peter for
the apostleship of the circumcision worked also in him for
the nations, for the uncircumcision.

In verse 9 Paul goes on to say, "And perceiving the
grace given to me, James and Cephas and John, who were
reputed to be pillars, gave to me and to Barnabas the right
hand of fellowship that we should go to the nations, and
they to the circumcision." In the listing of the apostles,

Peter was mentioned first (Matt. 10:2; Mark 3:16; Luke 6:14; Acts 1:13). However, here James is mentioned first. This indicates that the foremost leading one in the church at this time was not Peter, but James the brother of the Lord (Gal. 1:19). This is confirmed by Acts 15:13-21, where James, not Peter, was the authority to give the final decisive word in the conference held in Jerusalem. It must be that James came to the forefront to take the lead among the apostles because of Peter's weakness shown in not holding the truth of the gospel, as illustrated by Paul in verses 11 through 14. Hence, both in Galatians 2:12 and Acts 21:18, James was considered the representative of the church in Jerusalem and of the apostles. This is strong proof that Peter was not always the foremost leader of the church. This also implies that leadership in the church is not organizational and perpetual, but it is spiritual and fluctuates according to the spiritual condition of the leading ones. It strongly refutes the assertion of Catholicism that Peter was the only successor of Christ in the administration of the church.

H. Opposing Peter to His Face

Because Paul was honest, faithful, frank, and bold, he opposed Peter to his face when Peter was not faithful to the truth of the gospel. In 2:11 Paul says, "But when Cephas came to Antioch I opposed him to his face, because he was to be condemned." As we shall see, Peter was not faithful to the vision he had received concerning the Gentiles. When he was in Antioch, he not only played politics, but also acted in a hypocritical manner. For this reason, Paul opposed him.

II. THE UNFAITHFULNESS OF PETER

In 2:11-14 Peter's unfaithfulness to the truth of the gospel is exposed. In referring to this, we are not siding with Paul against Peter; we are simply speaking the facts.

A. Having Eaten with Those of the Uncircumcision

When I first read these verses, I was shocked. I could hardly believe what I was reading. But since these verses were written by Paul, they must be true. I found it hard to believe that one who had been with the Lord Jesus for three and a half years and who had seen the vision in Acts 10 regarding the abolition of the Levitical diet could practice such hypocrisy. Nevertheless, in Antioch Peter did just this. No wonder he lost his place of leadership. He was disqualified because he was not faithful to the vision he had seen. He did not keep the truth according to the vision he had received from the Lord.

In 2:12 we see that before certain ones came from James, Peter ate with those of the nations. This was against the customary practice of the Jews in keeping the observances of their law. If eating with those of the nations was wrong, Peter should not have done it in the first place. Since he ate with them, he indicated that it was proper to do so.

B. Shrinking Back and Separating Himself, Fearing Those of the Circumcision

When certain ones came from James, Peter "shrank back and separated himself, fearing those of the circumcision." The phrase "from James" means from the church in Jerusalem. This is another indication that at that time James, not Peter, was the first among the apostles and elders in Jerusalem. The fact that Peter shrank back proves that he was very weak in the pure Christian faith. He had received an exceedingly clear vision from the heavens concerning fellowship with the Gentiles, and he took the lead to put that vision into practice in Acts 10. What weakness and backsliding to shrink from eating with Gentile believers out of fear of those of the circumcision! No wonder he lost the leadership among the apostles.

In verse 12 Paul specifically points out that Peter feared

those of the circumcision. This indicates that in Jerusalem there was an atmosphere that strongly favored the observance of circumcision. Probably all the Jewish believers in Jerusalem, including Peter, were still in favor of this practice.

C. The Rest of the Jews Joining Him in Hypocrisy

In verse 13 Paul says, "And the rest of the Jews joined him in hypocrisy." When the leading one backslid, the rest easily followed. It is almost incredible that Peter, the leading apostle, practiced hypocrisy in relation to the truth of the gospel.

At least twice in the New Testament we are told that Peter took the lead in a negative way and that others followed him. In John 21 Peter led the way to go fishing. In this he was followed by some of the other disciples. Here in Galatians 2 Peter practiced hypocrisy, and others followed him.

D. Barnabas Carried Away by Their Hypocrisy

Paul points out that even Barnabas was carried away by their hypocrisy. Barnabas participated in Paul's first journey to preach the gospel to the Gentiles and to raise up the Gentile churches. Even one who had so much fellowship with the Gentile believers was carried away by Peter's hypocrisy. What a negative influence Peter exerted upon others! Surely he deserved to lose his leadership.

Although there was a prevailing atmosphere in favor of circumcision, Peter should not have been subdued. The Lord had shown him an impressive vision, and he should not have forgotten it. Nevertheless, even though he did not forget the vision, he behaved in a hypocritical way with respect to eating with the Gentiles.

E. Not Walking Straightforwardly in Relationship to the Truth of the Gospel

Because Peter and the others were hypocritical, Paul

rebuked him when he "saw that they did not walk straight-forwardly in relation to the truth of the gospel" (v. 14). Peter was absolutely wrong, and Paul rebuked him to his face. He would not allow the clear truth of the gospel to be damaged. Probably Paul was the only one with the boldness to rebuke a leading apostle such as Peter. Thank the Lord for Paul's faithfulness. If he had not been faithful there at Antioch, the truth of the gospel might have been blurred.

F. Compelling Those of the Nations to Live like Jews

In front of all, Paul said to Peter, "If you, being a Jew, live like the nations and not like the Jews, how is it that you compel the nations to live like Jews?" To live like the nations is to eat, live, and fellowship with the Gentiles. To live like Jews, or to Judaize (Gk.), is not to eat or have fellowship with the Gentiles.

We praise the Lord that through Paul's faithfulness the truth of the gospel was preserved. Today it is crystal clear according to the New Testament that in Christ there is no circumcision. We have been set free from slavery under the law and from the bondage of circumcision. There is no need for us to keep the law or to be circumcised. Rather, we only need faith in Christ. Because of Paul's faithfulness and boldness, this truth was preserved and has remained clear for us today. We thank the Lord for this.

LIFE-STUDY OF GALATIANS

MESSAGE SEVEN

FREEDOM IN CHRIST
VERSUS SLAVERY UNDER LAW

Scripture Reading: Gal. 2:4; 4:24-25, 28, 30-31; 3:3, 21; 2:20a; 5:1

In the book of Galatians Paul presents a number of contrasts between things that are superior and things that are inferior. In a foregoing message we pointed out the contrast between God's Son and man's religion. In this message we shall consider another contrast: freedom in Christ versus slavery under law. Christ is versus law, and freedom is versus slavery. When we come to chapter three, we shall see the contrast between the Spirit and the flesh. To touch the depths of this book, we need to keep in mind the writer's practice of making contrasts.

In 2:4 Paul says, "And it was because of the false brothers, brought in secretly, who stole in to spy out our freedom which we have in Christ Jesus, that they might bring us into slavery." The King James Version renders the Greek word for slavery as bondage. Although this is not wrong, the root word in Greek means to be a slave. Hence, the thought here is not simply to be in bondage, but to be enslaved, to be held in slavery.

If we would understand the contrast between freedom in Christ and slavery under law, we need a proper definition of the terms freedom and slavery. As we read these terms in the Scriptures, we may take them for granted without having a proper and adequate understanding. In 2:4 Paul speaks of false brothers who stole in to spy out our freedom. Such strong negative terms as "false brothers," "stole in," and "spy out" should impress us with the fact that freedom in Christ is a great matter. Otherwise, the

Judaizers, the false brothers, would not have crept in to spy out this freedom.

What is this freedom in Christ? First, freedom in Christ implies liberation from obligation. Because we are free in Christ, we are no longer obligated to the law and its ordinances, practices, and regulations. Anyone who tries to keep the law makes himself a debtor to the ordinances, practices, and regulations of the law. Hence, if you try to keep the law, you will place yourself under slavery and you will serve the law as a slave. Freedom in Christ, however, liberates us from all such obligation.

Second, freedom in Christ includes satisfaction with a rich supply. If we are free outwardly but do not have anything to support us or satisfy us, this freedom is not genuine. Proper freedom is not only liberation from obligation; it is also full satisfaction because of an adequate supply and support.

Third, to be free in Christ is to enjoy rest. Those who still observe the Sabbath day do not have true rest because their efforts to keep the Sabbath place them under a heavy burden. But in Christ we have true rest.

Fourth, freedom in Christ implies the enjoyment of Christ. Because we are free in Him, we enjoy all that He is. Real freedom in Christ is the full enjoyment of the living Christ.

If we would have a proper definition of freedom in Christ, a definition that matches our experience, we need to see that such a freedom involves liberation from obligations, satisfaction through the Lord's rich supply, genuine rest, and the enjoyment of Christ. Those who have this kind of freedom are not enslaved by anything. Although Satan may sometimes put us into a difficult situation, we can still be at rest. We need not be enslaved by any situation. Instead, we can enjoy the Lord. This means that we are free in the depths of our being. This is our freedom in Christ.

As you consider this description of freedom in Christ, you will find that it corresponds to your experience with the Lord. Our experience may differ in degree, but it does not differ in nature.

Freedom in Christ is a treasure. Satan, the subtle one, sent in the Judaizers to spy out this freedom and to deprive the Galatian believers of this treasure. He wanted to take away their liberation from obligation and their satisfaction, their rest, and their enjoyment of Christ.

Once we have a proper understanding of freedom in Christ, it is easy to understand what slavery is. It is the opposite of freedom. Slavery under law obligates us to the law with its commandments, ordinances, practices, and regulations. However, no one can fulfill the requirements of the law. Most of the Ten Commandments control people outwardly. But the commandment related to coveting exercises an inward control. We may be able to keep the other commandments, but not this one. We simply cannot escape the greediness within us. For example, we may see someone with a new pen that is better than ours. Deep within, we desire to have a pen just like it. This is covetousness.

Because we all have human shortcomings, we cannot fulfill the requirements of the law. Throughout history, only one person — the Lord Jesus — has kept the law. The requirements of the law are too heavy for us to fulfill. If we try to keep the law, we come under the yoke of the law. In Acts 15:10 Peter said, "Now therefore why tempt ye God, to put a yoke upon the neck of the disciples, which neither our fathers nor we were able to bear?" Slavery under law is this yoke.

To be enslaved under the law also means to be without satisfaction. Under the law there is no satisfaction because there is no supply. The law makes demands, but it offers no supply to meet those demands.

Furthermore, with slavery under law it is not possible for us to be at rest. In Matthew 11:28 the Lord Jesus said, "Come to Me all who labor and are burdened, and I will give you rest." This promise was spoken especially to those who were trying to keep the law. It refers in particular to

the labor of striving to keep the commandments of the law
and religious regulations. To have rest here means to be set
free from labor and burden under law and religion. In making this declaration, the Lord Jesus seemed to be saying,
"Come to Me, all who are burdened under the law, and I
will release you. I will set you free from the yoke of the law.
Under the law, you have no rest. True rest is found in Me."

Finally, with slavery under law there is no enjoyment of
Christ. Those who place themselves under obligation to the
law have no satisfaction, rest, or enjoyment.

If we consider this contrast between freedom in Christ
and slavery under law, we shall be full of praise to the
Lord. In Christ we have been liberated from all manner of
obligation. In Him we also have satisfaction, rest, and
enjoyment. This freedom in Christ is versus slavery under
law. Many of us can testify that we have such liberation,
satisfaction, rest, and enjoyment.

Concerning New Testament truth, Galatians is a more
basic book than Colossians. Colossians deals with Christian experience, but Galatians touches the basic truths of
the New Testament. Galatians is even more basic than
Romans. Galatians is the most basic book with respect to
God's New Testament economy. This book is unique in its
revelation of God's economy.

The slavery under law spoken of in Galatians is not the
same as the slavery of the children of Israel under Pharaoh.
These two kinds of slavery should not be confused. Egypt
was satanic, whereas the law is spiritual and was given by
God. Realizing this distinction will help us to be impressed
with the fact that no other New Testament book presents
the basic truths in the way Galatians does.

I. SLAVERY UNDER LAW

A. The Law, Typified by Hagar, Having No Position
in God's Promise and Grace

We need to see something further concerning slavery
under law. The law was typified by Hagar, Abraham's con-

cubine, who had no proper standing. This indicates that in God's promise and grace, the law has no position (4:24-25). As Abraham's wife, Sarah had the proper position in God's promise and grace. The wife could even tell Abraham to cast out the maidservant and her son. This shows that the law typified by Hagar has no position in God's promise and grace.

The Seventh-Day Adventists need to hear such a word. In obligating themselves to keep the Sabbath, they place themselves in the position of a concubine. When they do this, they have no position in God's grace.

B. The Law Unable to Give Life

In 3:21 Paul spoke like a skillful debater: "If a law was given which was able to give life, righteousness would have indeed been of the law." Because the law is composed of dead letters, it cannot give life.

Since the law is not able to give life, the law cannot produce sons. It can only produce slaves. Ishmael was not a proper son of Abraham; he was a slave. Hagar was not able to produce a son to be Abraham's heir. Because Ishmael's mother was a maidservant, Ishmael also was a slave. All those who endeavor to keep the law, such as the Seventh-Day Adventists, are today's Ishmaels brought forth by Hagar.

C. Slaves under Law
Striving to Keep the Law by the Flesh

Those who strive to keep the law do so, not by the Spirit, but by their flesh. For this reason, they do not participate in God's promise and have no enjoyment of life in grace by the Spirit (3:3). Life, grace, and the Spirit have nothing to do with the keeping of the law. The law does not have life, it does not give grace, and it does not depend on the Spirit. Hence, in the keeping of the law we have no life, grace, or Spirit. Instead, we have only our striving in the flesh.

II. FREEDOM IN CHRIST

A. Christ, Being the Life-giving Spirit, Imparting Life by Grace

As we consider the matter of freedom in Christ, we need to see that Christ as the life-giving Spirit imparts life by grace. This grace is typified by Sarah, the freewoman (2:20a; 4:31). As we have pointed out a number of times, grace is God processed to be our enjoyment. In 1:15 Paul says that God called him through His grace. This indicates that when God called us, He called us by Himself as the One processed to be our enjoyment. Christ as the life-giving Spirit imparts life into us by the Triune God who has been processed to become our enjoyment.

Many Christians regard grace merely as unmerited favor. According to this concept, to receive something from the Lord that we do not deserve is to receive grace. Many Christians think that the experience of grace is especially related to receiving material blessings. This understanding of grace is far from adequate. In John 1:14 we are told that when the Word (Christ) became flesh and tabernacled among us, He was full of grace. This surely does not mean that the Word which became flesh was full of material blessings. Furthermore, in John 1:16 we are told that of His fullness we have received grace upon grace. This definitely does not refer to receiving one material blessing upon another. The grace revealed in the New Testament is the very God incarnate who comes to us to be our enjoyment.

In 1 Corinthians 15:10 Paul says that he labored more than others. In this verse he also says that it was not he who labored, but the grace of God which was with him. This indicates that the grace which was with Paul was actually God Himself. Christ imparts life into our being by the Triune God processed to be our enjoyment. This is grace.

Grace is typified by Sarah, who also typifies God's promise. As we have pointed out, Hagar, the concubine, typifies the law. When we come to chapter four, we shall see that these women are an allegory signifying two covenants that bring forth two kinds of children. The grace typified by Sarah is the means Christ uses to impart Himself into us as life. This is absolutely different from law.

B. Life, Imparted by Christ,
Producing Sons Like Isaac
to Inherit God's Promise

The life imparted by Christ produces sons like Isaac, sons of the freewoman, who inherit God's promise (4:28, 30-31). When we received Christ as life, we became sons of God to inherit the blessing promised by God for the fulfillment of God's purpose.

C. Sons of Promise
Participating in God's Grace of Life,
Enjoying Freedom of Life

As sons of promise, we participate in God's grace of life and thereby enjoy the freedom of life (5:1). This means that we have liberation from obligation, and we have satisfaction, rest, and the enjoyment of Christ. This is the freedom that is versus slavery under law.

Galatians 2:4 presents the basic contrast between freedom in Christ and slavery under law. This indicates the fact that the book of Galatians gives us a number of basic truths and principles so that we may know God's New Testament economy in a proper way. Some saints in the Lord's recovery still may not be clear about God's New Testament economy. These messages on Galatians should help all of us to know God's economy in a basic way.

It is crucial for us to understand the basic terms, truths, and principles presented in Galatians. Thus far, we have covered two basic matters. The first is God's Son versus man's religion; the second is freedom in Christ versus slavery under law. We need to know the Son of God and also man's religion and tradition. We also must know the contrast between freedom in Christ and slavery under law.

Praise the Lord for our freedom in Christ! We are not in slavery under law — we enjoy freedom in Christ. We are free from obligation, and we have satisfaction, rest, and enjoyment in Christ.

LIFE-STUDY OF GALATIANS

THE TRUTH OF THE GOSPEL

Scripture Reading: Gal. 2:5b, 14a, 16, 19-20a; 3:11, 23-25; 4:2; 6:15

In 2:5 and 14 Paul speaks of the truth of the gospel. The word truth in these verses does not mean the doctrine or teaching of the gospel; it denotes the reality of the gospel. Although Galatians is a short book, it affords us a complete revelation of the reality of the gospel. This revelation, however, is given not in detail, but in certain basic principles. Therefore, in this message we shall cover the truth of the gospel revealed in these basic principles.

I. MAN NOT JUSTIFIED BY WORKS OF LAW

The first aspect of the truth of the gospel is that fallen man cannot be justified by works of law. In 2:16 Paul says, "Knowing that a man is not justified by works of law." At the end of this verse Paul declares, "By works of law no flesh shall be justified." The word flesh in 2:16 means fallen man who has become flesh (Gen. 6:3). No such man will be justified by works of law. Furthermore, in 3:11 Paul goes on to say, "Now that by law no one is justified before God is evident." In these verses Paul tells us clearly that no one is justified by works of law.

The Seventh-Day Adventists insist on strict observance of the Sabbath. However, they seem to forget that by endeavoring to keep the law with respect to the Sabbath, they make themselves debtors to keep all the commandments. The New Testament says that if we keep all the commandments except one, we transgress the whole law (James 2:10). Romans 7 proves that we cannot keep all the commandments. In verse 7 Paul refers to the commandment about coveting: "I had not known coveting except the

law had said, You shall not covet." Then in verse 8 he goes
on to say, "But sin, taking occasion through the commandment, wrought in me coveting of every kind." The
more Paul tried to keep this commandment, the more he
failed. This indicates that it is impossible for fallen man to
keep all of God's commandments. How ridiculous it is to go
back to the law and try to keep it! We simply do not have
the ability to keep the law. As Paul says in Romans 7:14,
the law is spiritual, but we are fleshly, sold under sin.
Therefore, by works of law shall no flesh be justified.

II. LAW BEING THE CUSTODIAN
TO KEEP GOD'S CHOSEN PEOPLE UNTIL CHRIST CAME

Since it is not possible for fallen man to keep the law,
we may ask why the law was given. It was not God's intention in giving the law that man should keep it. When God
gave the law, He knew that man would not be able to keep
it. God's purpose in giving the law was to use it as a custodian to keep His people until Christ came (3:23-24; 4:2).
God's intention was to use the law as a fold in which to
keep His sheep.

Perhaps you are wondering why Christ did not come
earlier than He did. Why did He not come at the time of
Moses? If Christ had come sixteen hundred years earlier,
there would have been no need for the law. Why did He not
come before the law was given? The best way to answer
this question is to turn to the Scriptures. Romans 3:19 and
20 say, "Now we know that whatever things the law says it
speaks to those who are under the law, that every mouth
may be stopped and all the world may become subject to
the judgment of God; because by the works of law no flesh
shall be justified before Him; for by law is knowledge of
sin."

In Galatians 3:19 Paul asks, "Why then the law?" In
the same verse he answers his own question: "It was added
because of transgressions." The law was given to expose
what man is and where man is. The best way for man to be
exposed is to cause his situation to be seen in the light of
God's attributes. The Ten Commandments are composed

mainly of four divine attributes: holiness, righteousness, light, and love. God is holy and righteous; He is also light and love. If you look into the Ten Commandments, you will see that they embody the divine holiness, righteousness, light, and love. For this reason, the law became God's testimony. In other words, the Ten Commandments testify that God is holy and righteous and that God is light and love. God used this testimony to expose man. As man stands before this testimony, his sinfulness is exposed.

When the law was given, the children of Israel promised to obey God's commandments (Exo. 19:8). Before the children of Israel responded in this way, the atmosphere around Mount Sinai was not threatening. But when the people declared that they would keep God's commandments, the atmosphere changed and became terrifying. God exercised His holiness, and the people were not allowed to approach further. Frightened by the manifestation of God's holiness, the people asked Moses to go to God on their behalf. This indicates that the function of the law is to expose fallen mankind.

As the law functions to expose people, it keeps them. Thus, the law was used by God as a custodian to keep His people just as a fold keeps a flock of sheep during the winter or during a storm. The time before the coming of Christ can be compared to a winter season. Hence, God used the law as a fold in which to guard the people. In their blindness the Judaizers thought that the law had been given for them to keep. They did not realize that the law was given to guard God's people in custody. Paul makes this basic principle clear in Galatians 3:23. "But before faith came we were guarded under law, being shut up unto the faith which was about to be revealed." In verse 24 he goes on to say, "So the law has become our child-conductor unto Christ, that we might be justified by faith." These verses reveal clearly that the law functions as a custodian. As it exposed man's transgression, it guarded God's people until Christ came.

Now that Christ has come, the law is over. But the foolish Judaizers wanted to go back to the law and try to keep it. They did not realize that the law has a dispensational function. When this function has been fulfilled, the law should not remain any longer. The stubborn Judaizers did not know God's purpose in giving the law. Therefore, even after Christ came, they held to the law. This is against the basic principle of God's economy.

III. LAW BEING OVER AFTER CHRIST CAME

In 3:25 Paul says, "But faith having come, we are no longer under a child-conductor." Since Christ has come, the law is over. The Seventh-Day Adventists need to learn this basic truth. Now that Christ has come, God's purpose in giving the law has been fulfilled. The law has handed God's people over to Christ. It is rebellion against God's economy to snatch the people away from Christ and lead them back to the law. We must be bold to tell the Seventh-Day Adventists that, as Christians, we must not go back to the law. The law has fulfilled its purpose.

IV. UNDER GOD'S NEW TESTAMENT ECONOMY

A. Man Justified by Faith in Christ

Under God's New Testament economy, we are not to keep the law. On the contrary, we are justified by faith in Christ (2:16). We may be so familiar with the expression "justified by faith in Christ" that we take it for granted. But what actually is faith in Christ, and what does it mean to be justified by faith in Christ? Faith in Christ denotes an organic union through believing. The proper preaching of the gospel is not the preaching of a doctrine; it is the preaching of the Person of the Son of God. The Son of God is the embodiment of the Father and is realized as the Spirit. To preach the gospel is to preach this Person. Whenever we preach the gospel, we must impress those who hear us with the living Person of the Son of God. No matter what the subject of our gospel message may be, the focal point of our preaching must be this living Person.

The faith in Christ by which believers are justified is related to their appreciation of the Person of the Son of

God. For example, in Hong Kong there are salesmen who are skillful in presenting jade and its values to people. The more they talk about jade, the more the listeners spontaneously appreciate jade. This appreciation can be compared to what we mean by faith. In our preaching of the gospel we must present Christ as the real jade. We need to present Christ as the most precious One to people. The more we describe Him and speak of His preciousness, the more something will be infused into the being of the listeners. This infusion will become their faith, and this faith will cause them to respond to our preaching. In this way they will appreciate the Person we present to them. This appreciation is their faith in Christ. Out of their appreciation for the Lord Jesus, they will want to possess Him. The Christ who has been preached to them will become in them the faith by which they believe. Faith is Christ preached into us to become our capacity to believe through our appreciation of Him.

When I was young, I heard a very precious gospel message. Although I had been in Christianity for years, I had never heard such a message. After hearing that message, my heart was captured, for some precious element had been infused into my being. I did not try to believe, but I had a spontaneous appreciation for the Lord Jesus. I was willing to give up the world in order to have Him. This is faith.

We may quote Hebrews 11:1, but still have only a doctrinal definition of faith. The genuine experiential definition of faith is that faith is the preciousness of Jesus infused into us. Through such an infusion, we spontaneously have faith in the Lord Jesus. This definition of faith matches our experience. The teaching of doctrine did not impress us with the preciousness of the Person of the Son of God. But one day we heard a living message filled with the preciousness of Christ. When this preciousness was infused into us through the preaching of the gospel, we spontaneously began to appreciate the Lord Jesus and to believe in Him. We said, "Lord Jesus, I love You. I treasure You." This is what it means to have faith in Christ.

This faith creates an organic union in which we and Christ are one. Therefore, the expression "by faith in Christ" actually denotes an organic union accomplished by believing in Christ. The term "in Christ" refers to this organic union. Before we believed in Christ, there was a great separation between us and Christ. We were we, and Christ was Christ. But through believing we were joined to Christ and became one with Him. Now we are in Christ, and Christ is in us. This is an organic union, a union in life.

This union is illustrated by the grafting of a branch of one tree into another tree. Through faith in Christ we are grafted into Christ. Through this process of spiritual grafting, two lives are grafted and become one.

Many Christians have a shallow understanding of justification by faith. How could Christ be our righteousness if we were not organically united to Him? It is by means of our organic union with Christ that God can reckon Christ as our righteousness. Because we and Christ are one, whatever belongs to Him is ours. This is the basis upon which God counts Christ as our righteousness.

Marriage is a helpful illustration of this, although it is inadequate. Suppose a poor woman is united in marriage to a wealthy man. Through this union she participates in the wealth of her husband. In like manner, through our organic union with Christ, we share whatever Christ is and has. As soon as this union takes place, in the eyes of God Christ becomes us, and we become one with Him. Only in this way can we be justified before God.

Many Christians have a mere doctrinal understanding of justification by faith. According to their concept, Christ is the just One, the righteous One on the throne in the presence of God. When we believe in Christ, God reckons Christ to be our righteousness. This understanding of justification is very shallow. As we have pointed out, in order to be justified by faith in Christ, we need to believe in the Lord Jesus out of an appreciation of His preciousness. As Christ's preciousness is infused into us through the preaching of the gospel, we spontaneously appreciate the Lord and call on Him. This is genuine believing. Through such a believing we and Christ become one. Therefore, God must reckon Him as our righteousness.

When we believed in the Lord Jesus, we had this kind of experience, although we did not have the terminology to explain it. When we heard the gospel, we began to sense the Lord's preciousness. This gave rise to the living faith that joined us to Christ organically. From that time onward, Christ and we became one in life and in reality. Therefore, justification by faith is not merely a matter of position. It is also an organic matter, a matter in life. The organic union with Christ is accomplished spontaneously through the living faith produced by our appreciation of Him. This is to be justified by faith in Christ.

B. Man Having Life and Living by Faith

In God's New Testament economy, man also has life by faith and lives by faith. In 3:11 Paul says, "The just by faith shall live." The word "live" here implies to have life. As a result of the organic union, we have life in us. Furthermore, we live by the faith which is our appreciation of the precious Lord Jesus. We not only have life, but we also live by this life.

C. Man Being Dead to Law
That He Might Live to God

In 2:19 Paul says, "For I through law have died to law that I might live to God." It is very difficult to explain in doctrine what it means to die to the law so that we might live to God. It is most helpful to consider this matter in the light of our experience. Our Christian experience proves that as soon as our organic union with Christ took place, we had the sense that we were dead to the world, to sin, to the self, and to all the obligations of the law. At the same time, we were conscious of the fact that we were alive to God. Probably when we first realized this, we had neither the knowledge nor the terminology to explain it. Perhaps you said, "Lord Jesus, from now on I don't care for anything other than You. I don't care for my education, my work, or my future. I don't even care for my family or my own life.

Lord Jesus, I care only for You." This is to be dead to everything in order to live to God.

D. Man Having Christ Living in Him

As those who are dead to the law and alive to God, we have Christ living in us. In 2:20 Paul says, "I have been crucified with Christ, and it is no longer I who live, but Christ lives in me." This also is a basic aspect of the truth of the gospel.

E. Man Being a New Creation

Another aspect of the truth of the gospel is that in Christ man is to be a new creation. Galatians 6:15 says, "For neither is circumcision anything nor uncircumcision, but a new creation." The new creation is the mingling of God with man. The new creation takes place when the Triune God in Christ through the Spirit is wrought into our being. This is the mingling of divinity with humanity. Living in this new creation far surpasses trying to keep the law. How foolish the Galatian believers were in going back to the law! They should remain in Christ by faith. In this union with Christ, Christ lives in us, and we become a new creation. Although we remain God's creature, we are nonetheless mingled with God the Creator. Having become one with the Creator, His life becomes our life, and our living becomes His living. This mingling produces a new creation. This is not accomplished by works of law, but by faith in Christ.

LIFE-STUDY OF GALATIANS

DEAD TO LAW BUT LIVING TO GOD

Scripture Reading: Gal. 2:19-20; 3:3; 5:16, 25; Rom. 7:4, 6; 6:4, 8, 10

This message is a continuation of the foregoing message on the truth of the gospel. The crucial point in that message was the organic union with Christ which takes place spontaneously when we believe in Christ. In this message we shall go on to see that we have died to law so that we might live to God (2:19).

ORGANIC UNION

How can we die to law in order to live to God? Galatians 2:19 indicates that we have already died to law. According to your experience, have you actually died to law, or is this simply a matter of doctrine to you? Furthermore, how can we live to God? If we would answer these questions, we must know the truth, the reality, of the gospel. If we are not actually organically united with Christ but are in ourselves, then we are neither dead to law nor are we living to God. Apart from the organic union with Christ, we cannot live to God. On the contrary, we shall be alive to many things other than God.

The concept of organic union is implied in Romans 7. In this chapter Paul uses the illustration of married life. Marriage is a union of life. In this union the wife is one with the husband, and the husband is one with the wife. In Romans 7:4 Paul speaks of our being married to Christ: "So that, my brothers, you also have been made dead to the law through the body of Christ, that you might marry another, even Him Who has been raised from among the dead." According to this verse, we have been married to the resurrected Christ. Between Him as the Bridegroom and us as the Bride, there is a wonderful union. We are one with Him in person, name, life, and existence. This shows that our Christian life is a life of organic oneness with Christ.

In Romans 11 Paul goes on to use another illustration — the grafting of a branch from one tree into another tree. In Romans 11:17-24 Paul uses the illustration of branches from a wild olive tree being grafted into a cultivated olive tree. As a result of grafting, the branches from the wild olive tree and the cultivated olive tree grow together organically. We, branches of the wild olive tree, have been grafted into Christ, the cultivated olive tree.

Some may say that the cultivated olive tree in Romans 11 refers to Israel. Although this is correct, it is also true that in the Bible the real Israel is always identified with Christ, and Christ with the real Israel. In the eyes of God, there are not two trees on earth. There is just one tree, the olive tree which includes Christ and God's chosen people. Once we were wild olive branches, but now we have been grafted into Christ. This illustration indicates that the Christian life is not an exchanged life, the exchange of a lower life for a higher one, but a grafted life, the grafting of the human life into the life of Christ. After a branch has been grafted into another tree, it no longer lives by itself. On the contrary, it lives by the tree into which it has been grafted.

CUTTING AND JOINING

In the matter of grafting, there are two main aspects: cutting and joining or uniting. Without the cutting, there cannot be any grafting. If the branch from one tree is to be grafted into another tree, the branch must firstly be cut. After the cutting occurs, the joining or union takes place. This union is organic. Therefore, in grafting we have the cutting, the joining, and the organic union. The cutting corresponds to the death of Christ, and the uniting, to the resurrection of Christ. In the death of Christ our old life was cut off, and in Christ's resurrection we were united to Him for further growth. The experience of the death of Christ causes us to die to the law, whereas resurrection enables us to live to God. Hence, to be dead to the law and alive to God implies the death and resurrection of Christ. Only by being grafted into Christ can we be one with Him in His death and resurrection.

In ourselves it is not possible for us to die to law or live to God. However, when the preciousness of the Lord Jesus was infused into us and we began to appreciate Him, we were grafted into Him. On the one hand, we were cut; on the other hand, we were joined to Christ in His resurrection life. After this union took place, we were organically united with Christ. Now we should simply live in this organic union. On the negative side, we have been cut in Christ's death; on the positive side, we have been united to Christ in His resurrection. In this cutting we died not only to the law, but to everything other than God. According to Galatians 6, we are dead to the world, particularly to the religious world, through the crucifixion of Christ (vv. 13-14). By the all-inclusive cutting of Christ's all-inclusive death on the cross, we are dead to everything other than God. Because we have been grafted into Christ, His experience has become our history. When He died on the cross, we died in Him. When He was crucified, we were cut off from the wild olive tree. This means that we were cut off from the self, the flesh, the world, religion, and the law with its ordinances. Furthermore, because we have been grafted into Christ, His resurrection has also become our history. Therefore, we can strongly declare that with Christ we have been crucified, buried, and resurrected. What a wonderful history we have!

Having been cut off from everything other than God, we are dead to religion, including Judaism, Catholicism, and Protestantism. One aspect of our history includes the crucifixion by which we have been cut off from everything other than God. But the other aspect of this history includes the resurrection in which we have been united to the Triune God. In this union, we are absolutely one with the Triune God.

It is crucial that we all see this vision. However, few Christians have seen it. If we see the vision of this organic union, our living will be changed. We shall realize that we have been cut off from the old source and united to the living One.

BY FAITH IN CHRIST

It is by faith in Christ that we enter into such an organic union with Him. We have pointed out that faith is the appreciation of Jesus. This appreciation is implied even in Galatians 2:20. In this verse we see that we have been crucified with Christ. This refers to one aspect of our history. We also see that Christ lives in us and that the life that we now live in the flesh we live in the faith of the Son of God who loved us and gave Himself for us. It is significant that in this verse Paul specifically refers to the Son of God as the One "who loved me." If we do not have any consciousness of Christ's love for us, we shall not be able to have faith in Him. Living faith comes from our sense of His love. This indicates that the faith by which we believe in Him is related to our appreciation of His loveliness. As we sense His preciousness, spontaneously an appreciation for Him wells up within us. This appreciation is our faith. When Paul referred to the Son of God as the One who "loved me and gave Himself for me," he was filled with appreciation for the Lord Jesus. This appreciation is the very faith about which he speaks in this verse. The life he lived in the flesh he lived in this faith, the faith of the Son of God.

Whenever we say from the depths of our heart, "Lord Jesus, I love You," our faith is strengthened. Our organic union with Christ is strengthened also. Furthermore, we sense that we have been cut away from sin, the world, the flesh, and religion. Some who have seen the light concerning the church have not been willing to give up the denominations. But one day they told the Lord how much they loved Him. Spontaneously they had the sense within that they should give up their association with the denominations. Because their organic union with Christ was strengthened, they experienced more cutting. The more we say, "Lord Jesus, I love You," the more we sense that we have been cut off from everything other than Christ.

As we tell the Lord Jesus that we love Him, we experience the operation of genuine faith that is implied in our appreciation of Him. By this faith we realize our union with Christ. In this union we realize that His history is our history; with Christ we have been crucified, buried, and resurrected. We are dead to everything other than God, and we are living to God.

How foolish the Galatians were in turning from the Lord to the law! Did they not realize that they had been cut off from the law and joined to the living God? Through the organic union we are released from slavery under law. In this union we enjoy the freedom that is ours in Christ.

LIVING TO OUR OWN LAWS

In your experience do you know that you are dead to law and alive to God? I do not have much assurance that many Christians realize this. Few Christians are actually living to God. For the most part, they are still living to something other than God, especially to their own kind of law. Instead of caring for God, we may care for our type of law. Different persons have different laws. The young people have their law, and the older ones have their law. This is the reason that the older ones unconsciously condemn the young ones. This condemnation comes from their law. Instead of living to God, we live to our kind of law. We have been cut off from the Mosaic law, but in our experience we have not been cut off from our own law. The fact that we still have our own laws indicates that our love for the Lord is not adequate. We are still short in our appreciation of Him. This lack weakens our faith. However, when our love for the Lord Jesus increases, our condemnation of others will decrease. If the older saints have a greater appreciation of the Lord, their condemnation of the young people will be swallowed up.

Just as the older saints have the tendency to condemn the young ones, the young ones may not appreciate the older ones. Suppose the young saints and the older saints come together for a prayer meeting. It will be difficult for them to work together. Either the older ones will be prevailing and dominating, or the younger ones will. The reason for this problem is that the older ones have their law and the younger ones have theirs.

It is easy for us to proclaim in a doctrinal way that we have died to law and that we are now living to God. Our practical experience, however, may be quite different. We may not have died to certain things, and we may not be living to God. Therefore, we need to turn to the Lord and receive more infusion from Him. As a result, we shall have a greater love and appreciation for Him. This will strengthen our faith, which will then operate in us to strengthen our union with Christ. As our organic union with Him is strengthened, we shall experience more cutting. If we all have this experience, in the meetings we shall no longer have the consciousness of the difference between the young ones and the old ones. Instead, we all shall realize that we have been cut away from everything other than the Triune God. Then in the prayer meetings we shall function, not conscious of our age, but in the organic union in which we are truly dead to law and living to God.

In this message I am concerned with experience, not with passing on mere knowledge. If we condemn others, we are deficient in our love for the Lord. Instead of living to God, we live to our own law. Those who do not fulfill the requirements of our law we condemn. However, if our appreciation of the Lord is adequate, the operating faith will work to strengthen our union with Christ, and we shall experience more cutting. Then in reality we shall have no law. We shall truly be dead to law and alive to God.

LIVING IN THE ORGANIC UNION

In 2:19 Paul says, "For I through law have died to law that I might live to God." The law requires me, a sinner, to die, and according to that requirement Christ died for me and with me. Hence, I have died in Christ and with Christ through the law. Therefore, the obligation under the law, the relationship to the law, has been terminated. To live to God means to be obligated to God in the divine life. In Christ's death we are through with the law, and in His resurrection we are responsible to God in the resurrection life.

We have become dead to the law so that we may live to God. As long as we still hold to any kind of law, whether the Mosaic law or our self-made law, we cannot live to God. However, when we are cut off from the law by means of the organic union with Christ, we spontaneously live to God.

To be dead to law means that we have been discharged from the law in which we were held. Romans 7:6 says, "But now we are discharged from the law, having died to that in which we were held." Having been liberated from obligation to the law, we may now walk in newness of life (Rom. 6:4). However, walking in newness of life depends upon the cutting we experience in the organic union with Christ. The more we experience the cutting, the more we live to God and walk in newness of life.

Because we have died to law, we are no longer obligated to keep the law by the striving of the flesh (Gal. 3:3). Whenever we have a certain self-made law, we always strive to keep it by the strength of the flesh, not by the Spirit.

To be living unto God is to be obligated to God in the divine life, to be responsible to God in the resurrection life. In the organic union with Christ, we experience resurrection life. In this resurrection life we are held to God spontaneously and are obligated to Him. This also depends on the organic union.

Because we have been crucified with Christ, it is no longer we who live, but Christ lives in us. We no longer live in the old man, the natural man. Rather, Christ lives in us. Then in resurrection we live in the faith of the Son of God. To live in the faith of the Son of God means to live in the organic union with the Son of God which comes through our believing in Him.

We live to God with Christ (Rom. 6:8, 10) and through the Spirit (Gal. 5:16, 25). This is the enjoyment of the processed Triune God in our experience. This experience depends on our appreciation of the loveliness and preciousness of the Lord Jesus.

PRESENTING CHRIST IN HIS LOVELINESS

In principle, in preaching the gospel we should be like the top salesmen, who are able to present something precious in a way that others will appreciate it. We need the proper salesmanship. The Lord Jesus is infinitely precious, but our presentation of Him is not always adequate. Since we do not know how to present the loveliness of the Lord Jesus in a proper way, it is difficult for those who listen to our gospel preaching to have faith in Him. But if we present Him adequately, others will be infused with His preciousness, and they will spontaneously appreciate Him. This appreciation will become their faith which will operate in them to unite them with the Lord Jesus organically. Here in this organic union we are dead to the law and alive to God.

LIFE-STUDY OF GALATIANS

MESSAGE TEN

NO LONGER I,
BUT CHRIST LIVING IN ME

Scripture Reading: Gal. 2:19-20; Rom. 6:6a, 8; 2 Cor. 5:14-15; 1 Cor. 15:45b; 2 Cor. 3:17; John 6:57b; Phil. 1:21a

Galatians 2:20 is a familiar verse. In this verse is one of the basic items of God's New Testament economy: no longer I, but Christ living in me. According to God's economy, we should no longer live; rather, Christ should live in us. This is a basic aspect of the truth of the gospel. However, most Christians do not have the proper and adequate understanding of what it means to say no longer I, but Christ living in me.

NOT AN EXCHANGED LIFE

Because this has not been made clear, some Christians, including certain Christian teachers, think that 2:20 speaks of what has been called an exchanged life. According to this concept, we are replaced by Christ. Christ comes in, and we go out. According to the concept of an exchanged life, our life is pitiful, and the life of Christ is far better. Therefore, we should exchange our life for Christ's life. As we shall see, this concept is wrong.

Galatians 2:20 does not speak of an exchanged life. Here Paul says, "No longer I who live, but Christ lives in me." Then he goes on to say, "And the life which I now live in the flesh I live in faith, the faith of the Son of God." On the one hand, Paul says, "It is no longer I who live"; on the other hand, he says, "I live." If you consider this verse as a whole, you will see that there is no thought of an exchanged

life. Here what is presented is not an exchange; rather, it is
a profound mystery.

We have pointed out that the book of Galatians reveals
the basic truths of God's New Testament economy. Among
these basic truths, the most basic one is found in 2:20.
Because the truth of no longer I, but Christ living in me is
so basic, it is also mysterious; and because it is mysterious, it has not been properly understood by Christians
throughout the centuries. Therefore, we look to the Lord
that He would make this basic truth clear to us.

<h2 style="text-align:center">THE OLD "I" AND THE NEW "I"</h2>

We have pointed out that in this verse Paul says, on
the one hand, "no longer I" and, on the other hand, "I
live." How can we reconcile this? Once again I wish to
point out that this is not an exchange of life. The way to
interpret the Bible properly is by the Bible itself. This
means that other verses are needed if we are to understand
this verse. Romans 6:6 tells us that our old man has been
crucified with Christ. This verse helps us to see that the
very I who has been crucified with Christ is the old "I," the
old man. As regenerated people, we have both an old "I"
and a new "I." The old "I" has been terminated, but the
new "I" lives. In Galatians 2:20 we have both the old "I"
and the new "I." The old "I" has been crucified with
Christ, terminated. Therefore, Paul can say, "no longer I."
However, the new "I" still lives. For this reason, Paul can
say, "I live."

Now we must go on to see the difference between the
old "I" and the new "I." Because we are so familiar with
2:20, we may take this verse for granted and assume that
we understand it. But what is the difference between the
old "I" and the new "I"? According to the natural understanding, some would say that the old "I" is evil, whereas
the new "I" is good. This concept of the difference between
the old "I" and the new "I" must be rejected. The old "I"
had nothing of God in it, whereas the new "I" has received
the divine life. The old "I" has become a new "I" because

God as life has been added to it. The "I" that has been terminated is the "I" that was without divinity. The "I" who still lives is the "I" into which God has been added. There is a great difference here. The old "I," the "I" without God, has been terminated. But the new "I" still lives, the "I" that came into being when the old "I" was resurrected and had God added to it. On the one hand, Paul has been terminated. But, on the other hand, a resurrected Paul, one with God as his life, still lives.

Because of their rejection of God's light many Christians are blind to this understanding of 2:20. If they heard such a word about the old "I" and the new "I," they would reject it. Their rejection, however, would be completely without ground. As genuine Christians, they have been regenerated. When a person is regenerated, he is not annihilated or destroyed. To be regenerated means to have God added into us. In regeneration, we who once did not have God in us now have Him added to us. The very "I" who did not have God in it is over. This is the old "I," the old man, who has been crucified with Christ. But from the time that we began to appreciate the Lord Jesus and the operating faith began to work in us, this faith brought the processed Triune God into us and added Him to our being. From that time onward, we have had a new "I," an "I" with God in it. Hence, the new "I" is the old "I" which has become an "I" resurrected with God added to it. Praise the Lord that the old "I" has been terminated and the new "I" now lives!

LIVING WITH CHRIST

In 2:20 Paul says, "Christ lives in me." According to the concept of an exchanged life, our life is terminated and Christ lives. But we need a more thorough understanding of what it means to say that Christ lives *in us*. It is rather easy to understand that Christ lives. But it is difficult to understand how Christ lives in us. This does not mean that I have been crucified and live no longer, and that Christ lives instead of me. On the one hand, Paul said, "no longer I"; on the other hand, he said, "Christ lives in me." The phrase "in me" is of great importance. Yes, it is Christ who lives, but it is in us that He lives.

In order to understand how Christ can live in us, we need to turn to John 14. Before His death and resurrection, the Lord Jesus said to the disciples, "Because I live, you shall live also" (v. 19). Christ lives in us by causing us to live with Him. Christ does not live alone. He lives in us and with us. He lives by enabling us to live with Him. In a very real sense, if we do not live with Him, He cannot live in us. We have not been altogether ruled out, and our life has not been exchanged for the divine life. We continue to exist, but we exist with the Triune God. The Triune God who now dwells within us causes us to live with Christ. Hence, Christ lives in us through our living with Him.

ONE LIFE AND ONE LIVING

Once again the illustration of grafting helps our understanding. After a branch has been grafted into a productive tree, the branch continues to live. However, it lives not by itself, but by the tree into which it has been grafted. Furthermore, the tree lives in the branch which has been grafted into it. The branch now lives a grafted life. This means that it lives, not by itself, but by the life of the tree into which it has been grafted. Furthermore, this other life, the life of the productive tree, does not live by itself, but through the branch grafted into it. The life of the tree lives in the branch. Eventually, the branch and the tree have one life with one living. In the same principle, we and Christ also have one life and one living.

In John 6:57 the Lord Jesus said, "As the living Father sent Me, and I live because of the Father, so he who eats Me shall also live because of Me." The Son did not live by Himself. However, this does not mean that the Son was set aside and ceased to exist. The Son, of course, continued to exist, but He did not live His own life. Instead, He lived the life of the Father. In this way the Son and the Father had one life and one living. They shared the same life and had the same living.

It is the same in our relationship with Christ today. We and Christ do not have two lives. Rather, we have one life and one living. We live by Him, and He lives in us. If we do not live, He does not live; and if He does not live, we cannot live. On the one hand, we are terminated; on the other hand, we continue to exist, but we do not live without Him. Christ lives within us, and we live with Him. Therefore, we and He have one life and one living.

DEAD TO THE LAW

Galatians 2:20 explains how through law we have died to law. When Christ was crucified, we were included in Him according to God's economy. This is an accomplished fact. We have died in Christ through His death, but now He lives in us through His resurrection. His living in us is entirely by His being the life-giving Spirit (1 Cor. 15:45b). This point is fully developed in the following chapters of Galatians, where the Spirit is presented and emphasized as the very One whom we have received as life and in whom we should live.

LIVING CHRIST

"I," the natural person, is inclined to keep the law that I might be perfect (Phil. 3:6), but God wants me to live Christ that God may be expressed in me through Him (Phil. 1:20-21). Hence, God's economy is that "I" be crucified in Christ's death and Christ live in me in His resurrection. To keep the law is to exalt it above all things in my life; to live Christ is to make Him the center in my life, even to make Him everything to me. The law was used by God to keep His chosen people in custody for Christ for a period of time (Gal. 3:23), and eventually to conduct them to Christ (3:24) that they might receive Him as life and live Him as God's expression. Since Christ has come, the function of the law has been terminated; therefore, Christ must replace the law in my life for the fulfillment of God's eternal purpose.

CHRIST AND THE SON OF GOD

In 2:20 Paul speaks both of Christ and of the Son of God. The title "Christ" mainly denotes Christ's mission to carry out God's plan. "The Son of God" denotes Christ's Person to impart God's life into us. Hence, the faith in which we live God's life is in the Son of God, the life-imparting One. The Son of God loved us and purposely gave Himself for us that He might impart the divine life into us.

The life which we now live in the flesh is not *bios,* the physical life, not *psuche,* the soulish life, but *zoe,* the spiritual and divine life.

THE FAITH WHICH OPERATES IN US

Paul says that the life we now live in the flesh we live in faith, the faith of the Son of God. We live the divine life, not by sight or by feeling in the way we live the physical and soulish life. The divine life, which is the spiritual life in our spirit, is lived by the exercise of faith stimulated by the presence of the life-giving Spirit.

In speaking of faith, Paul refers to "the faith of the Son of God." What is the meaning of the little word "of" here? This word implies that the faith mentioned in this verse is the Son of God's faith, the faith which He Himself possesses. However, in interpreting this verse, we and many others have said that this phrase actually means faith *in* the Son of God. Nevertheless, the Greek does not use the preposition "in" here. I have spent a good deal of time trying to understand this matter. After consulting the writings of a number of leading authorities, I have become fully convinced that here Paul is not speaking of the Son's faith, but of faith in the Son. However, we still need to explain why in this verse, as well as in 2:16 and 3:22, Paul does not use the preposition "in." We cannot gain a proper understanding of this simply by studying the Scripture in black and white letters. We also need to consider our experience.

Paul wrote the book of Galatians both according to

truth and according to his experience. According to our
Christian experience, the genuine living faith which oper-
ates in us is not only *in* Christ, but also *of* Christ. Hence,
Paul's meaning here actually is "the faith of and in
Christ." Paul's thought is that the faith is both of Christ
and in Christ.

We have pointed out that faith is our appreciation of
what the Lord is and of what He has done for us. We have
also pointed out that genuine faith is Christ Himself
infused into us to become our ability to believe in Him.
After the Lord has been infused into us, He spontaneously
becomes our faith. On the one hand, this faith is *of* Christ;
on the other hand, it is *in* Christ. However, it is too simple
merely to say that this faith is Christ. We need to say that
it is Christ revealed to us and infused into us. Faith is
related not only to the Christ who has been infused into us,
but also to the Christ who is infusing Himself into us. As
Christ operates in us, He becomes our faith. This faith is of
Him and also in Him.

APPRECIATING THE LORD JESUS

Proof that the faith in 2:20 is both the faith of Christ
and the faith in Christ is found in Paul's words at the end
of the verse. He concludes the verse by referring to the Son
of God as the One "Who loved me and gave Himself for
me." In writing these words, Paul was filled with appreciation of the Lord Jesus. Otherwise, at the end of such a
long verse there would have been no need for him to speak
of Christ loving him and having given Himself for him. He
could have concluded with the expression, "the faith of the
Son of God." But as he was speaking of the way he now
lived, his heart was filled with gratitude and appreciation.
Faith comes from such an appreciation of the Lord Jesus.
The faith in Christ and the faith of Christ issues from the
appreciation of Christ.

In 2 Corinthians 5:14 and 15 Paul says, "For the love of
Christ constraineth us; because we thus judge, that if one
died for all, then were all dead: and that he died for all,

that they which live should not henceforth live unto themselves, but unto him which died for them, and rose again." As we consider these verses, we can see that Paul's faith came from an appreciation for the constraining love of Christ. The more we appreciate Christ's constraining love, the more faith we shall have. This faith is not produced by our own ability or activity. Rather, it is produced by the working in us of the very Christ whom we appreciate. In our appreciation for the Lord Jesus, we shall say, "Lord Jesus, I love You and I treasure You." As we speak such words to the Lord, He operates within us and becomes our faith. This faith brings about an organic union in which we and Christ are truly one.

I would like to tell you a true story which confirms the point that the faith which operates in us comes from our appreciation of the Lord Jesus. During the Boxer Rebellion in China, hundreds of Christians were martyred. One day in Peking, the old capital of China, the Boxers were parading down the street. Sitting in the back of a wagon was a young Christian woman who was being led away to be executed. She was surrounded by executioners with swords in their hands. The atmosphere was terrifying, filled with the shoutings of the Boxers. Nevertheless, her face was glowing as she was singing praises to the Lord. The stores were closed because of the rioting. However, a young man was observing this scene through a crack at the front of a store. Deeply impressed with the young woman's glowing face, happiness, and songs of praise, he decided at that moment that he would find out the truth about the Christian faith. Later, he did learn the truth and became a believer in Christ. Eventually, he gave up his business and became a preacher. One day, when he was visiting my home town, he told me this story of how he had become a Christian.

The point here is that this young woman could be filled with praises in the midst of such a terrifying situation because faith was working within her. She was filled with appreciation of the Lord Jesus. Because she loved Him so much, He spontaneously became the faith within her. This faith produced an organic union in which she was joined to the Lord. This organic union is a basic and crucial aspect of God's New Testament economy.

A REVELATION OF GOD'S ECONOMY

The Galatians had turned from God's economy and had gone back to the law, which they were trying to keep by the efforts of the flesh. But when we endeavor to keep the law in this way, we are far off from God. God's economy is not that we try to keep the law in the strength of our flesh. His economy is to work Himself into us. The Triune God has become the processed God. Through incarnation, Christ came in the flesh to fulfill the law and then to set it aside. Through His resurrection, Christ has become the life-giving Spirit, ready to enter into us. God's New Testament economy is for the processed Triune God to be wrought into us to become our life and our very being. If we see this, we shall be able to proclaim that we have been crucified with Christ and that we live no longer. Nevertheless Christ lives in us, and we live by the faith that is in Him and of Him. Our old person has been crucified, but the new person, the new "I," still lives. Now we live by faith in the Son of God and of the Son of God, a faith that produces an organic union in which we and Christ are one. There is no comparison between keeping the law and such an organic union.

Galatians 2:20 is a revelation of God's economy. In His economy God's intention is for the processed Triune God to be wrought into our being to make us a new person, a new "I." The old person, the old "I," the "I" without God, is over; but the new person, the new "I," the "I" with the Triune God in it, still lives. We live with Christ and by Christ. Furthermore, we live by faith, which is the means to bring us into oneness with Him. In this organic union we are one with the Lord, for we have one life and one living with Him. When we live, He lives. He lives in us, and we live with Him.

THE VISION OF CHRIST LIVING IN US

I believe that now we can understand what it means to say that Christ lives in us and that the life which we now live, we live by the faith of the Son of God who loved us and gave Himself for us. The experience portrayed in this verse implies that God in His Trinity has been processed. After Christ was incarnated, He lived on earth and then was crucified, buried, and resurrected. In resurrection He became the life-giving Spirit. After His ascension, Christ was crowned, enthroned, and made the Lord of all. On the day of Pentecost, He descended as the Spirit upon His Body. From that time until now, He has been working and moving on earth, seeking those who will appreciate Him and call on His name. Whenever we call on the Lord Jesus out of our appreciation of Him, He comes into us and becomes the living faith which operates in us and brings us into an organic union with Him. In this union we can truly say, "I have been crucified with Christ, and it is no longer I who live, but Christ lives in me; and the life which I now live in the flesh I live in faith, the faith of the Son of God, Who loved me and gave Himself for me." This is God's New Testament economy. I hope that this vision will be infused into all the saints.

I can testify that because I have seen this heavenly vision, nothing can move me. I am willing to give my whole life for such a vision of God's economy. The old person has been crucified with Christ, and Christ now lives in me, the new person. The life I now live, I live by faith, the faith of the Son of God and in the Son of God, who loved me and gave Himself for me. Here we have the mingling of the Triune God with the tripartite man. How wonderful!

LIFE-STUDY OF GALATIANS

MESSAGE ELEVEN

NOT NULLIFYING THE GRACE OF GOD

Scripture Reading: Gal. 2:21, 16, 20a; 3:3; 4:21; 5:2, 4, 16, 24-25; John 1:17; 6:57b; 15:4-5; 1 Cor. 6:17; 15:45b; 2 Cor. 3:17; Rom. 5:17-18, 21; 1 Tim. 1:14

In 2:21 Paul says, "I do not nullify the grace of God." If we consider this verse in context, we see that to nullify the grace of God means that in our experience we do not have Christ living in us. In verse 20 Paul says, "It is no longer I who live, but Christ lives in me." Then he goes on to say that he does not nullify the grace of God. This is a strong indication that for us as believers to nullify the grace of God is for us to deny Christ the opportunity to live in us. The grace of God is simply the living Christ Himself. To allow Christ to live in us is to enjoy the grace of God. But not to allow Him to live in us is to nullify God's grace.

GRACE IN THE NEW TESTAMENT

It is important for us to find out the genuine and proper significance of the grace of God in the New Testament. In the Old Testament there is actually no mention of God's grace. The word grace used in the Old Testament means favor. John 1:17 tells us that grace came with Jesus Christ. Before the incarnation of the Son of God, grace had not come. Grace came when the Lord Jesus came. Prior to that time, the law had been given through Moses. The promise of grace had also been made to Abraham; it was given before the law was. First, God gave the promise of grace to Abraham. Then, four hundred thirty years later, the law was given at Mount Sinai through Moses. Approximately

another fifteen hundred years passed before grace came
with Jesus Christ, with the incarnated Son of God.

According to John 1:1 and 14, the Word that was in the
beginning with God and which was God became flesh and
tabernacled among us, full of grace and reality. Verse 16
says, "For of His fullness we all received, and grace upon
grace." Since grace came with Jesus Christ, grace was not
yet present in the Old Testament.

Now we must give a definition of grace. Grace is God in
His Trinity processed through incarnation, human living,
crucifixion, resurrection, and ascension to be everything to
us. After passing through such a long process, the Triune
God has become everything to us. He is our redemption,
salvation, life, and sanctification. Having been processed
to become the all-inclusive life-giving Spirit, the Triune
God Himself is our grace.

GREATER THAN THE LAW

If we would understand grace as revealed in the New
Testament, we need a clear view of the New Testament as
a whole. Grace is a matter of tremendous significance. To
the Jews, the giving of the law through Moses was a great
event. The fact that the coming of grace is contrasted with
the giving of the law indicates that grace is greater than the
law. As far as the Jews were concerned, apart from God
Himself nothing was greater than the law. But John 1:17
indicates that grace is greater than the law. The law was
given, but grace came.

THE SON OF GOD LIVING IN US

According to the concept of many Christians, God's
grace is mainly a matter of material blessing. At the end of
the year, some Christians gather together to count the
blessings God has bestowed on them during that year and
to thank Him for His great grace in sending these blessings. Then they proceed to thank the Lord for things such
as a large home and new clothes. Such a concept of grace is

much too poor! The Apostle Paul would count such things as dung, not as grace.

We have pointed out that, according to John 1:17, grace is greater than the law. Surely God Himself is higher than the law. However, if God remains objective to us, in our experience He will not be greater than the law. In order to be greater than the law to us, the Triune God must be subjective. Hence, in the New Testament, grace denotes the Triune God processed to become everything to us and to live in us. Nothing can surpass the living in us of the processed, all-inclusive life-giving Spirit.

We have pointed out that in 2:20 Paul says that he has been crucified with Christ and that Christ lives in him. Then in verse 21 he goes on to say that he does not nullify the grace of God. This indicates that the grace of God is the Son of God living in us. Certainly this is much greater than the law. The Son of God was incarnated not only to live on earth, to be crucified, to be resurrected, and to ascend into the heavens; He also came to live in us. This is grace.

To go back to the law is to reject this grace. It is to reject the very Son of God who now lives in us. This is to nullify the grace of God. However, if we remain in Christ, enjoying Him as everything to us, we do not nullify the grace of God.

All of Paul's Epistles begin and end with a word about grace. This is also true of the book of Revelation. In Revelation 1:4 John writes to the seven churches which are in Asia, "Grace to you"; and in 22:21, he concludes with the words, "The grace of the Lord Jesus be with all the saints." Paul closes the Epistle to the Galatians by saying, "The grace of our Lord Jesus Christ be with your spirit, brothers." If grace were a matter of material blessing, how could grace be with our spirit? Grace is not physical or material; it is divine and spiritual. Actually, as we have pointed out emphatically, grace is God Himself in a subjective way to be everything for our enjoyment. I hope that all the saints could grasp this definition of grace in a clear way.

WHAT GRACE DOES FOR US

Let us now consider according to the New Testament what this grace has done for us and what it will do for us. Although man was created in God's image and likeness in order to express Him and represent Him, man became fallen. In the fall man not only did something wrong outwardly, but the very nature of sin was injected into man's being. Hence, outwardly we are sinful, and inwardly we are evil. Before the righteous God, our conduct is sinful, and in the eyes of the holy God, our nature is evil. Furthermore, there is nothing we can do about our situation. It is utterly foolish for fallen man to go to the law and endeavor to keep it. Even if we could keep the law, what would we do about our evil nature? How we must praise God for His grace and for what it has done for us! First, the Triune God became incarnated to live on earth to fulfill the requirements of God's righteous and holy law. Having fulfilled the law's requirements, He went to the cross and died there for our sins as our substitute. Through His death Christ has redeemed us. Therefore, redemption is the first item of what God's grace has accomplished for us.

After accomplishing redemption through His death, Christ was resurrected from among the dead to release the divine life from within Him. In resurrection He has become the life-giving Spirit to be received by those who will appreciate Him, love Him, believe in Him, call on Him, and repent. As soon as a sinner responds to Him in this way, He as the life-giving Spirit enters into that one and through regeneration is born in him. Is this not an aspect of God's grace? It is the second item of what God's grace has done for us.

Third, from the time of our regeneration, Christ has been dwelling in our spirit to live in us and with us. By living in us, Christ enables us to have the kind of living that satisfies God. In His grace, Christ lives in us and with us.

As Christ lives within us, He also ministers all His riches into our being in order to sanctify us, transform us, and make us sons of God in reality and practicality. In this way, we enjoy full sonship.

Fifth, at the appointed time, Christ will come back and saturate our physical body with His element. This will cause our body to be transfigured into a glorious body, a body which is the same as Christ's resurrection body. Certainly this is another aspect of God's grace. By saturating us, Christ will glorify us and be glorified in us. He will bring us all into His glory, where we shall be exactly the same as He is, in spirit, soul, and body.

Finally, in eternity and for eternity we shall enjoy Christ as the living water and as the tree of life.

This description of what the grace of God is to us covers the entire New Testament from the opening of Matthew to the end of Revelation. The Triune God — the Father, the Son, and the Spirit — has been processed through incarnation, human living, crucifixion, resurrection, and ascension in order to come into us, to be one with us, and to be everything to us. Now He is our redemption, salvation, life, living, sanctification, and transformation, and He will become our conformation, our glorification, and our eternity. This is the portion of the saints in light (Col. 1:12).

ENJOYING GRACE

We cannot enjoy God's grace in full in one day or even in a lifetime. It will take eternity for us to have the full enjoyment of this grace. This is the very grace which came when the Lord Jesus came, and this is the grace we need day by day. Praise the Lord that this is the grace we find by approaching the throne of grace daily to meet our timely need. Every morning we should look to the Lord and pray, "Lord, grant me Your grace today. I need today's portion of Your grace. May grace be with me and with all my brothers and sisters." Oh, we all need to pray like this! Then we shall experience grace, the grace who is the very Triune God processed to become the all-inclusive life-giving Spirit for our enjoyment.

In 2:21 Paul says, "For if righteousness is through the

law, then Christ has died for nothing." Christ died for us that we may have righteousness in Him, through which we may receive the divine life (Rom. 5:18, 21). This righteousness is not through the law, but through the death of Christ. If righteousness is through the law, Christ has died without cause, for nothing. But righteousness is through Christ's death, which has separated us from law. Now, according to Romans 5:17, we who "receive the abundance of grace and of the gift of righteousness shall reign in life through the One, Jesus Christ." Grace enables us to reign in life.

It is the grace of God that Christ has imparted the divine life into us through the life-giving Spirit. Not to live by this Spirit is to nullify the grace of God. To nullify God's grace is to reject the processed Triune God who has become the all-inclusive life-giving Spirit. The Judaizers wanted the Galatian believers to go back to the law. To return to the law is to nullify the grace of God. It is to deny and reject the processed Triune God. Furthermore, it is also to fail to experience and enjoy such a processed God. By this we can see that to nullify the grace of God by returning to the law is extremely serious.

GOD'S ECONOMY

In their blindness the Judaizers were foolish. If they had seen what the grace of God is, they would not have been Judaizers. But because they were blind, they zealously endeavored to turn people away from Christ. They failed to realize that it is not God's economy that His chosen people keep the law. God's economy is for His people to enjoy the Triune God who has been processed to become the life-giving Spirit through incarnation, human living, crucifixion, resurrection, and ascension. In His economy God intends that His people enjoy Himself as such a Triune God and become one with Him. Then His people will be one in the divine life to express God corporately. This corporate expression of the Triune God is the church life. The ultimate issue of this will be the New

Jerusalem, the corporate expression of the Triune God in eternity.

If we see this vision of God's economy, how could we go back to the law? How could we turn away from the Triune God who has been processed to become our grace? No wonder Paul said that the Galatians were foolish. In their folly they were nullifying the grace of God.

STANDING IN GRACE

If we would be those who do not nullify the grace of God, we need to abide in Christ (John 15:4-5). To abide in Christ is to remain in the processed Triune God. Furthermore, we need to enjoy Christ, especially by eating Him (John 6:57b). Then we should go on to be one spirit with Christ (1 Cor. 6:17), to walk in the Spirit (Gal. 5:16, 25), to deny the natural "I" (2:20), and to abandon the flesh (5:24). We should not be distracted by things such as the law, circumcision, the Sabbath, and dietary regulations. Rather, we should enjoy Christ and live with Him in one spirit. If we walk in spirit, deny the natural "I," and abandon the flesh, we shall be those who do not nullify the grace of God.

We praise the Lord that in His recovery we are enjoying and experiencing His grace. Many Christians, however, are not in the experience of this grace. In Romans 5:2 Paul says that by faith we have access into this grace in which we stand. Let us stand fast in the grace into which we have entered.

LIFE-STUDY OF GALATIANS

CHRIST CRUCIFIED

Scripture Reading: Gal. 3:1; 1:4; 2:20; 3:13; 2:21, 19; 5:24; 6:14-15

In the foregoing message we considered the grace of God. In this message we come to Christ crucified. Christ crucified has a great deal to do with our enjoyment of God's grace. The enjoyment of the grace of God is altogether dependent on the crucifixion of Christ.

In 3:1 Paul says, "O foolish Galatians, who has bewitched you, before whose eyes Jesus Christ was openly portrayed crucified?" The crucifixion of Christ indicates that all the requirements of the law have been fulfilled by the death of Christ, and that Christ through His death has released His life that it may be imparted into us in His resurrection to free us from bondage under the law. This was fully portrayed before the eyes of the Galatians in the word of the gospel. How could they neglect this and be bewitched, drifting back to the law? How foolish!

Before the eyes of the Galatians, Christ had openly been portrayed crucified. Paul wondered how the Galatian believers could forget such a portrait. Those who go back to the law have nothing to do with such a crucified Christ. If God wants us to keep the law and if we are able to keep it, then there was no need for Christ to be crucified. For this reason, Paul declares in 2:21, "If righteousness is through law, then Christ has died for nothing." Galatians 3:1 is the direct continuation of 2:21. Christ certainly was not crucified without cause. On the contrary, He was crucified for a very great cause. In fact, the cross is the center of God's operation in His economy, just as Christ Himself is the center of God's economy. In the carrying out of God's economy, the cross is the center. Without Christ, God's economy has no center, and without the cross of Christ the operation of God's economy is without a center. Thus, the carrying out of God's economy wholly depends on the cross of Christ. The cross is the center of God's operation in the universe to carry out His economy.

This is the reason that in such a short book Paul many times refers to the cross. He constantly brings us back to the cross. In 2:21 Paul points out that Christ was not crucified for nothing. Then in 3:1 he goes on to remind the Galatians that the crucifixion of Christ was openly portrayed before their eyes. When Paul came to Galatia, he preached a crucified Christ. In order to be righteous, we need such a Christ. If we could have righteousness through keeping the law, then we would not need a crucified Christ. If this had been the case, there would have been no reason for Christ to die.

In 3:1 Paul brought the Galatians back to the cross. He wanted them to have a thorough look at the crucified Christ. In this message I am burdened that we also have such a view of Christ crucified. Therefore, let us consider the verses in Galatians which refer to the cross or to the death of Christ on the cross, and let us see all the important points in these verses.

I. TO GIVE HIMSELF FOR OUR SINS
THAT HE MIGHT RESCUE US
OUT OF THE PRESENT EVIL AGE

In 1:4 Paul says that Christ "gave Himself for our sins, that He might rescue us out of the present evil age, according to the will of our God and Father." Here we see that in His crucifixion Christ gave Himself for our sins. How foolish were the Galatians, and how stubborn and rebellious were the Judaizers! In returning to the law, they had no way to deal with their sins. In this book Paul seems to be saying, "You have committed many sins. What will you do about them? Apart from the death of Christ on the cross, there is no way to be redeemed from your sins."

Although Christ was crucified for our sins, the goal of His crucifixion was to "rescue us out of the present evil

age." Sins are devilish, whereas this age is satanic. We
have pointed out that the present age is the present section
of Satan's cosmos, his world system. As the Devil, God's
enemy is involved with sins; and as Satan, he is involved
with the evil age. Even if the Galatians and the Judaizers
could have been successful in keeping the law, how would
they have dealt with the Devil, Satan? Can you overcome
Satan? He is subtle, lurking behind sins and the evil age.
Apart from the crucifixion of Christ, we have no way to
deal with sins, behind which the Devil hides, or the evil
age, behind which Satan hides. Christ was crucified for our
sins that He might rescue us from this evil age. This indicates that only Christ can save us from the Devil and
Satan. Both sins and the evil age have been dealt with by
Christ crucified. He gave Himself for us on the cross
according to the will of God.

II. TO GIVE HIMSELF FOR US
THAT HE MIGHT IMPART LIFE TO US
AND LIVE IN US IN RESURRECTION
TO FREE US FROM THE BONDAGE UNDER LAW

Christ was crucified in order to give Himself for us that
He might impart life to us. This is altogether positive,
whereas dealing with sins and rescuing us from the evil age
are negative. On the positive side, Christ crucified imparts
the divine life to us so that He might live in us in resurrection to free us from bondage under law (2:20). Through
His death on the cross, Christ released His divine life and
imparted the divine life into us. This makes it possible for
Him to live in us in resurrection.

If Christ had not been crucified, it would not be possible for Him to come into us. A "raw," unprocessed Christ
cannot dwell in us. Before Christ could come into us and
live in us, He had to deal with our sins and with our fallen
nature. The old "I," the "I" without God, had to be dealt
with. To deal with sin and with our fallen nature, Christ
had to be crucified. Dealing with these negative things
opened the way for Christ to impart Himself into us as our

life and thereby to live in us. Thus, Christ's living in us is based upon His death on the cross.

Furthermore, the Christ who lives in us is a Christ in resurrection. If Christ had not been crucified, how could He have been resurrected? This would, of course, have been impossible. And if Christ were not in resurrection, He could not live in us. The only Christ who can dwell in us is a resurrected Christ, a processed Christ, a Christ who has passed through incarnation, human living, crucifixion, and resurrection. The process through which Christ has passed affords Him the ground and the way to enter into us and to live in us in His resurrection life. A "raw" Christ could never be life to us. The Christ who is our life and who lives in us is the processed Christ. Through His crucifixion He dealt with our sins and with our fallen nature. Now, based upon the work accomplished in His crucifixion, He lives in us in resurrection. This indicates clearly that the cross is the center of God's operation for the carrying out of His economy.

III. TO REDEEM US OUT OF THE CURSE OF THE LAW

Galatians 3:13 says, "Christ has redeemed us out of the curse of the law, having become a curse on our behalf; because it is written, Cursed is every one hanging on a tree." Christ as our substitute on the cross not only bore the curse for us, but also became a curse for us. The curse of the law issued from the sin of man (Gen. 3:17). When Christ took away our sin on the cross, He redeemed us out of the curse.

The Galatians surely were foolish in going back to the law. What did they expect to do about the curse of the law? As descendants of Adam, they were under the curse like everyone else. If we read Romans 5, we see that Adam brought us all under the curse. But the curse was not altogether official until the law was given. But the law now declares that all the fallen descendants of Adam are under the curse. In Galatians 3:13 Paul seemed to be telling the Galatians, "The law is not good to you, for it has made the curse official. The curse brought in by the fall of Adam has been made official by the law. You are very foolish to return to the law. The law condemns you and makes your curse official. But through His crucifixion, Christ has redeemed us out of the curse of the law. On the cross He was even made a curse for us."

Sin, the evil age, and the curse were all serious problems. Without the cross of Christ, how could God deal with these problems and carry out His economy? We certainly need Christ crucified. We need the Christ who has died on the cross to solve all these problems.

IV. TO FULFILL THE REQUIREMENT OF THE LAW THAT WE MAY HAVE RIGHTEOUSNESS IN HIM

Galatians 2:21 says, "I do not nullify the grace of God; for if righteousness is through law, then Christ has died for nothing." This verse indicates that Christ died to fulfill the requirements of the law that we may have righteousness in Him. In Adam we do not have righteousness; rather, we have a sinful nature. But Christ was crucified on the cross to fulfill all the requirements of God's holy and righteous law. Now we may have righteousness in Christ.

Some Christians have seen only that Christ died on the cross for our sins. They have not also seen that He died to become our righteousness. Dying for our sins is related to redemption, whereas dying to become our righteousness is related to justification. Redemption is on the negative side, but justification is on the positive side. The cross of Christ is both for redemption and justification. Through His death we have been redeemed from our sins, and through His death we have also obtained righteousness in Him.

V. TO MAKE US DEAD TO LAW THAT WE MIGHT LIVE TO GOD

In 2:19 Paul says, "For I through law have died to law that I might live to God." Apart from the crucifixion of Christ, there is no way for us to die to the law. Christ was crucified to make us dead to the law. Even if we in ourselves could die to the law, that type of death would not count in the eyes of God. The only death that matters in

His eyes is the death of Christ. Death in Adam is horrible, but the death of Christ is lovely and even lovable, for it accomplishes a great deal for us. Through Christ's death, we have become dead to the law so that we might live to God.

VI. TO HAVE US CRUCIFIED WITH HIM
THAT WE MAY BE ABLE TO CRUCIFY OUR FLESH

Through the crucifixion of Christ we have been crucified with Christ. This enables us to crucify our flesh with the passions and lusts (5:24). In other words, we have been crucified with Christ so that we may be able to crucify our flesh.

We all are troubled by the old man, the self, and the flesh. Romans 6:6 says that our old man, not our flesh, has been crucified with Christ. Galatians 5:24 says that those who are Christ's have crucified the flesh. This verse does not say that those who belong to Christ have crucified their old man. However, there is no verse which tells us that the self has been crucified with Christ. The "I" in 2:20 does not refer to the self; it denotes the old man, the person without God. Thus, our old man, not our self, has been crucified with Christ. Furthermore, according to 5:24, it is our flesh which must be crucified. Christ has crucified the old man, but we who belong to Christ must crucify the flesh. Our crucifying the flesh with its passions and lusts is based upon the fact that our old man has been crucified with Christ. Could we crucify our flesh if Christ had not been crucified? Certainly not!

We need to have a clear understanding concerning the old man, the self, and the flesh. There is no need for us to deal with the old man, for the old man has already been crucified with Christ. However, day by day we need to crucify our flesh. The problems in our daily living do not come from the old man, but from the flesh with its passions and lusts. Therefore, based upon the fact that our old man has already been dealt with through the death of Christ, we must go on to crucify our flesh in a practical way.

It is crucial to see the difference between Romans 6:6

and Galatians 5:24. In 5:24 Paul does not say that those who are Christ's have crucified the old man. He says that they have crucified the flesh. Furthermore, we need to see that no one can crucify himself. It is not possible to commit suicide by crucifixion. For this reason, it is not possible for us to crucify our old man, our old "I." Although we cannot crucify the old man, we can crucify the flesh. This is not suicide. The crucifixion of the old man had to be accomplished by someone else, but the crucifixion of the flesh must be carried out by us.

How then shall we deal with the self? We must deny the self through bearing the cross. The self is already on the cross. Let us leave it there and not allow it to come down. To cause the self to stay on the cross is to bear the cross.

Now we can see that if Christ had not been crucified, we would not have any basis or foundation for the crucifixion of our flesh. Furthermore, if Christ had not been crucified, we would have no place to leave the self. But since Christ has died on the cross, we can crucify our flesh, based on the fact that the old man has been crucified. Also, we have a place to leave the self. Whenever the self rises up, we need to say, "Pitiful self, go back to the cross and stay there. I do not allow you to come down from the cross and make proposals to me. Your place is the cross." This is the proper way to deny the self.

The cross of Christ is the basis both for the crucifixion of the flesh and the denial of the self. By means of Christ's resurrection life we can crucify the flesh and keep the self on the cross. When Christ was crucified, we were crucified also. Now in His resurrection life He lives in us, and we live in Him. With His crucifixion as the foundation, we are now able in Christ's resurrection life to crucify the flesh and deny the self.

VII. TO HAVE THE WORLD CRUCIFIED TO US AND US CRUCIFIED TO THE WORLD

Finally, Christ was crucified to have the world crucified to us and us to the world. This especially refers to the religious world. In 6:14 Paul declares, "But far be it from me to boast except in the cross of our Lord Jesus Christ, through Whom the world has been crucified to me and I to the world." The following verse indicates that the world in verse 14 refers mainly to the religious world. This religious world is the evil age from which we have been delivered through the cross of Christ.

To go back to the law is to turn away both from Christ and from the cross. To do this is to nullify the grace of God. It is of vital importance for us to see what the cross of Christ has accomplished for us. Through the cross Christ redeemed us from our sins, rescued us from the present evil age, and redeemed us from the curse of the law. Through the cross Christ has fulfilled the requirements of the law so that we may be righteous, and He has enabled us to be dead to the law so that we might live to God. Through Christ's crucifixion we now have the ground to crucify the flesh and the way to be separated from the world.

As we consider all these matters, we see that not one of them could be accomplished through keeping the law. Because the Galatians were endeavoring to keep the law, Paul considered them foolish and told them that they had been bewitched. In this Epistle Paul was bringing them back to the cross and encouraging them to behold Christ crucified. If we have a clear vision of Christ crucified, we shall never go back to the law. On the contrary, we shall put the law under our feet and remain with Christ who was crucified for us. This Christ is the center of God's economy, and the cross of Christ is the center of God's operation to carry out His economy. Today we have no need of the law. What we need is Christ and the cross.

LIFE-STUDY OF GALATIANS

MESSAGE THIRTEEN

CHRIST AND THE SPIRIT

Scripture Reading: Gal. 3:1-5, 13-14; 4:6; 1 Cor. 15:45b;
2 Cor. 3:17; Rom. 8:2, 9-10

Chapter three of Galatians is crucial, but it is also extremely difficult to understand. It is one of the most difficult chapters in the New Testament. Therefore, it is not easy to explain in a few sentences what this chapter reveals. As we read this important chapter, we should not take it for granted, assuming that we understand all the terms used by Paul. For example, in this chapter Paul refers to the hearing of faith (v. 2). We should not assume that we understand this term.

In 3:1—4:31 we see a basic contrast between the Spirit by faith and flesh by law. In this contrast we have two sets of opposites: the Spirit and the flesh as one set, and faith and law as another. The law goes along with the flesh, whereas faith accompanies the Spirit. Hence, the Spirit is by faith, and the law is by flesh.

The first two chapters of Galatians may be regarded somewhat as the outer edge of this book. Chapter three, however, is the center of the book, its inner core. In this central section of Galatians is presented the contrast between the Spirit and the flesh, and also the contrast between faith and law. Therefore, it is correct to say that the subject of chapters three and four is the Spirit by faith versus the flesh by law. To have this understanding of these chapters is to have something of great value. Apart from seeing this contrast, we have no way to understand what these chapters reveal.

As we come to 3:1-14, we see that the Spirit is the blessing of the promise by faith in Christ. Here we have the

Spirit, the blessing, the promise, the faith, and Christ. The
Spirit is the blessing, the blessing is of the promise, the
promise is by faith, and faith is in Christ. What does it
mean to say that the Spirit is the blessing and that the
blessing is of the promise? What does it mean that the
promise is by faith? Understanding such matters is not
easy. Nevertheless, these are the very matters to which we
must pay attention as we consider these chapters.

In 3:1-5 Paul refers to the Spirit three times. In verse 2
he asks, "Did you receive the Spirit by the works of law or
by the hearing of faith?" In verse 3 he goes on to ask, "Having begun by the Spirit, are you now being perfected by the
flesh?" Then in verse 5 Paul asks whether the Galatian
believers are supplied the Spirit by works of law or by the
hearing of faith. Therefore, the Spirit is a crucial matter in
3:1-5.

Another crucial matter is the hearing of faith. Paul
mentions the hearing of faith both with respect to receiving the Spirit (v. 2) and to God's supplying the Spirit
(v. 5). Both the receiving of the Spirit and the supplying of
the Spirit are related to the hearing of faith. Doctrinally
speaking, the hearing of faith is of greater importance here
than the Spirit, for Paul's point is the contrast between the
works of law and the hearing of faith. Although the hearing of faith is of such vital importance, it is neglected by
many readers of Galatians, who either ignore this matter or
take it for granted. Rarely does anyone seek to know what
actually is the hearing of faith.

In Romans 8:2 we see the relationship between the
Spirit of life and Christ: "For the law of the Spirit of life in
Christ Jesus has freed me from the law of sin and of
death." What does it mean to say that the Spirit of life is in
Christ? Traditional teaching would lead us to believe that
the Spirit and Christ are separate and distinct Persons.
But if the Spirit is a Person separate from Christ, how can
the Spirit be in Christ? Some Christian teachers say that
Christ the Son, the second Person of the Trinity, is sitting
on the throne in the heavens and that the Holy Spirit, the

third Person of the Trinity, is now working within us. In contrast to the traditional teaching that the Spirit and Christ are separate and distinct, the Bible tells us that the Spirit is in Christ.

The Lord's answer to Philip's question in John 14 helps us to understand this matter. When Philip said to Him, "Lord, show us the Father and it suffices us" (v. 8), the Lord answered, "Am I so long a time with you, and you have not known Me, Philip? He who has seen Me has seen the Father. How is it that you say, Show us the Father? Do you not believe that I am in the Father, and the Father is in Me? The words which I speak to you, I do not speak from Myself; but the Father Who abides in Me, He does His works" (vv. 9-10). The Lord's word indicates clearly that the Father and the Son are not two separate Persons. On the contrary, the Father is in the Son, and the Son is in the Father. They cannot be separated. Furthermore, the Son was sent *from with* the Father (John 6:46, Gk.). On the one hand, He was sent from God; on the other hand, He was always with God. The Son did not actually leave the Father; neither was the Father separated from the Son. Therefore, the Lord said, "Believe Me that I am in the Father and the Father in Me" (John 14:11).

The principle is the same concerning the relationship of Christ and the Spirit as the relationship between Christ the Son and the Father. The fact that the Spirit of life is in Christ means that an intrinsic relationship exists among the Three of the Godhead. The Son is the Son, and the Father is the Father. Nevertheless, the Father is in the Son, and the Son is in the Father. Likewise, while the Son is the Son and the Spirit is the Spirit, yet the Spirit is in the Son. This indicates that the Three of the Triune God cannot be separated.

A further indication of this truth is found in Romans 8:9-10. In these verses Paul says, "But you are not in the flesh, but in the spirit, if indeed the Spirit of God dwells in you. But if any one has not the Spirit of Christ, he is not of Him. And if Christ is in you, though the body is dead because of sin, yet the spirit is life because of righteousness." In these verses we read of the Spirit of God, the Spirit of Christ, and Christ. These titles all denote one reality — the all-inclusive Spirit. The Spirit of God is God, the Spirit of Christ is the Spirit of God, and Christ Himself is the Spirit of Christ. Christ is the Spirit of Christ, the Spirit of Christ is the Spirit of God, and the Spirit of God is God Himself. All these titles refer to the all-inclusive life-giving Spirit. This One is the Spirit of God, the Spirit of Christ, the Spirit of life, Christ, and God.

In Romans 8:2 and 9 there are three titles of the Spirit: the Spirit is the Spirit of life, the Spirit of God, and the Spirit of Christ. Hence, the Spirit is of life, of God, and of Christ. Certainly these titles do not refer to three Spirits. It is utterly wrong to say that the Spirit of life is separate from the Spirit of God or that the Spirit of God is distinct from the Spirit of Christ. On the contrary, the one Spirit is the Spirit of life, of God, and of Christ. Life, God, and Christ are not three separate entities or substances. Rather, life is God, God is Christ, and Christ is life. Therefore, the Spirit of life is the Spirit of God, and the Spirit of God is the Spirit of Christ. These three are one entity, the all-inclusive Spirit.

I. CHRIST AND THE SPIRIT BEING ONE

First Corinthians 15:45b says that the last Adam became a life-giving Spirit. Second Corinthians 3:17 tells us that now the Lord is the Spirit. The last Adam in 1 Corinthians 15:45b and the Lord in 2 Corinthians 3:17 both refer to Christ. This indicates clearly that today Christ and the Spirit are one.

II. CHRIST CRUCIFIED ON THE CROSS

In 3:1 Paul declares that before the eyes of the Galatian believers "Jesus Christ was openly portrayed crucified." The Lord was crucified on the cross as Christ, not as the Spirit. We cannot say that the Spirit was crucified for us. It was Christ who was crucified.

III. CHRIST ENTERING AS THE SPIRIT
INTO THE BELIEVERS

The Galatians through hearing the gospel believed in the crucified Christ, but they received the Spirit (3:2; 4:6). The One who was crucified on the cross was Christ, but the One who entered into the believers was the Spirit. In crucifixion for the believers' redemption He was Christ, but in the indwelling to be the believers' life He is the Spirit. This is the all-inclusive life-giving Spirit, who is the all-inclusive and ultimate blessing of the gospel. The believers receive such a divine Spirit by the hearing of faith, not by the works of law. He enters into the believers and lives in them, not by their keeping the law, but by their faith in the crucified and resurrected Christ.

We should not think that the One who died on the cross is different from the One who enters into us. The One who died for us is the very One who has entered into us as our life. When this One died on the cross, He died as Christ. When He enters into us to be our life, He comes in as the Spirit. In crucifixion for our redemption He was Christ (3:13). But in the indwelling to be our life He is the Spirit (Rom. 8:2, 9-10).

IV. THE SAVED ONES BELIEVING
IN THE CRUCIFIED AND RESURRECTED CHRIST,
BUT RECEIVING THE SPIRIT

We believe in the crucified and resurrected Christ, but we receive the Spirit (3:2). The title of the One in whom we believe is Christ, not the Spirit. However, when we believe in Christ, we receive the Spirit. Christ is the One who was crucified for the accomplishment of redemption and who was resurrected. Hence, we believe in Him. But when He comes into us, He comes in as the Spirit. In the function of redemption, His title is Christ, whereas in the function of life, His title is the Spirit. As the most important Person in the universe, Christ has more than one status. Although Christ and the Spirit are one, there is a difference in function, title, and status.

V. CHRIST IN THE REVELATION OF GOD'S ECONOMY AND THE SPIRIT IN OUR EXPERIENCE OF LIFE

In the revelation of God's economy in the first two chapters of Galatians, the emphasis is on Christ. But in our experience of life as presented in the last four chapters, the emphasis is on the Spirit. Have you noticed that in Galatians 1 and 2 there is no mention of the Spirit? However, verse after verse speaks of Christ. Beginning with 3:2, the Spirit is revealed. The Spirit in chapter three is the very Christ in chapter two. Do not think that the Spirit is separate from Christ. In the chapters which deal with the revelation of God's economy, we read of Christ, but in those chapters which unfold our experience of life, we read of the Spirit. On the one hand, Galatians gives us a revelation of God's economy; on the other hand, it affords us a revelation of our experience of life. The former is objective, whereas the latter is subjective. In the objective revelation of God's economy the emphasis is on Christ, but in the subjective experience of life the emphasis is on the Spirit.

VI. THE BELIEVERS RECEIVING THE SPIRIT AS THE ALL-INCLUSIVE AND ULTIMATE BLESSING OF THE GOSPEL

As believers, we have received the Spirit, the all-inclusive life-giving Spirit, as the all-inclusive and ultimate blessing of the gospel. According to the understanding of many Christians, the One they received when they believed in the Lord Jesus was only Christ, the Son of God. Not many realize that the One they received was not the objective Christ, but the subjective Spirit. Because many are not clear concerning this, they talk about a so-called second blessing, or about receiving the Spirit apart from regeneration. When some Christians learn that another has believed in Christ, they proceed to ask him if he has received the Holy Spirit. However, to be a genuine Christian is to believe in Christ and to receive the Spirit. To be a real Christian is to believe in Christ, and to believe in

Christ is to receive the Spirit. Nevertheless, those who regard Christ as separate and distinct from the Spirit may consider that it is possible to believe in Christ without receiving the Spirit. This is a serious misunderstanding! As we have pointed out again and again in this message, we simultaneously believe in Christ and receive the Spirit.

When certain Christians are asked if they have received the Spirit, they are not clear or do not know how to answer. They need to see that when we believed in the Lord Jesus, an organic union took place. At the very time of our conversion, a wonderful organic union between us and the Lord Jesus was accomplished. Because they are ignorant of the fact of such an organic union, they do not enjoy the Spirit as the ultimate blessing of the gospel. Instead of enjoying this blessing, they are distracted to regulations, doctrine, or to the study of the Bible in dead letters. Others may pursue what is called the second blessing or the outpouring of the Spirit with speaking in tongues. But in the four books which make up the heart of the divine revelation in the New Testament — Galatians, Ephesians, Philippians, and Colossians — nothing is said about tongues-speaking or about the outpouring of the Spirit. Instead, Paul places strong emphasis on the sealing of the Spirit, the earnest of the Spirit, and the foretaste of the Spirit. When we believed in the Lord Jesus, we were sealed with the Spirit. At the very moment the organic union took place, the earnest of the Spirit was given. In other words, when we believed in the Lord Jesus, we received the Spirit, and the Spirit became to us the ultimate blessing of the gospel.

The Judaizers were ignorant of this mysterious organic union with Christ, and the Galatian believers were not clear about it and were distracted from it. The same is true of many Christians today. Because so many believers do not realize what took place within them at the time they believed in the Lord Jesus, they are distracted and occupied with other things. Therefore, it is crucial for us to see what happened in us when we believed in the Lord. By means of an organic union we were grafted into the Triune

God. Now all the Triune God is, has done, has accomplished, and has obtained and attained has become our portion. Because the Judaizers were troubling the believers in Galatia and because the believers themselves were lacking in understanding, Paul was burdened to write this Epistle. He was especially burdened to cover the matters in chapter three. Every believer must be clear that Christ and the Spirit are one. This oneness is a mystery for our enjoyment.

LIFE-STUDY OF GALATIANS

HEARING OF FAITH
VERSUS WORKS OF LAW

Scripture Reading: Gal. 3:2, 5, 3, 20, 9, 14, 22-25; Rom. 7:10-11, 24; 8:2, 6, 10-11, 30

Galatians 3:2 says, "This only I wish to learn from you, Did you receive the Spirit by the works of law or by the hearing of faith?" Surely we have received the Spirit by the hearing of faith, not by the works of law.

In 3:5 Paul goes on to ask the Galatian believers, "He therefore Who is supplying to you the Spirit and doing works of power among you, is it by the works of law or by the hearing of faith?" God continues to supply the Spirit to us also through the hearing of faith, not at all by the works of law.

SUPPLYING AND RECEIVING

God's New Testament economy is a matter of supplying the Spirit and receiving the Spirit. On God's side, He supplies the Spirit; on our side, we receive the Spirit. The supplying of the Spirit and the receiving of the Spirit do not take place once for all. On the contrary, they are continual. According to 3:2, we have already received the Spirit. But according to 3:5, God continues to supply the Spirit to us. Day by day God supplies the Spirit, and day by day we receive this supply of the Spirit. Therefore, by our experience we know that the supplying of the Spirit and the receiving of the Spirit take place continually.

THE CONTRAST BETWEEN FAITH AND LAW

Both the supplying of the Spirit and the receiving of the Spirit are by the hearing of faith, not by the works of law.

The law was the basis for the relationship between man
and God in God's Old Testament economy (3:23); faith is
the unique requirement for man to contact God in His New
Testament economy (Heb. 11:6). Law is related to the flesh
(Rom. 7:5) and depends on the effort of the flesh, the very
flesh that is the expression of "I." Faith is related to the
Spirit, and trusts in the operation of the Spirit, the very
Spirit who is the realization of Christ. In the Old Testament, "I" and the flesh played an important role in keeping the law. In the New Testament, Christ and the Spirit
take over the position of "I" and the flesh, and faith
replaces law that we may live Christ by the Spirit. To keep
the law by the flesh is man's natural way; it is in the darkness of man's concept and results in death and wretched-
ness (Rom. 7:10-11, 24). To receive the Spirit by faith is
God's revealed way; it is in the light of God's revelation
and issues in life and glory (Rom. 8:2, 6, 10-11, 30). Hence,
we must treasure faith, not the works of law. It is by the
hearing of faith that we have received the Spirit that we
may participate in God's promised blessing and live
Christ.

In 3:22-25 we see a contrast between law and faith.
According to 3:23, "before faith came we were guarded
under law, being shut up unto the faith which was about to
be revealed." This verse indicates clearly that there was a
time when faith came and was revealed. According to
verses 24 and 25, now that faith has come we are no longer
under the law as our child-conductor. Faith and law cannot co-exist. Before faith came, we were under law. But
now that faith has come and has been revealed, this faith
replaces law.

FAITH AND GRACE

In fundamental Christianity it is commonly taught that
the law has been replaced by grace. Theological terms such
as the dispensation of law and the dispensation of grace are
used to point out this distinction. According to this understanding, the Old Testament was the dispensation of law,

whereas the New Testament is the dispensation of grace. Hence, grace is versus law and replaces law. But have you ever heard that faith has come to replace law and that faith is versus law? It is possible even to say that in the Old Testament there was a dispensation of law, but in the New Testament there is a dispensation of faith. The dispensation of grace is also the dispensation of faith. When grace came, faith came also. Both grace and faith came with the coming of Jesus Christ.

What a contrast there is between the works of law and the hearing of faith! We must distinguish between a working Christian and a hearing Christian. What kind of Christian are you? We all should declare that we are hearing Christians, not working Christians. To hear is a great blessing. In the meetings of the church we come together for the hearing of faith. By this hearing we receive the supply of the Spirit.

If we would understand the meaning of the hearing of faith, we need to know what faith is and also what grace is. Both grace and faith refer to the same thing. Grace is on God's side, but faith is on our side. As we have pointed out, grace is the Triune God processed to be everything to us. As we hear of this grace, we spontaneously have faith.

If I were preaching the gospel to primitive people who had never heard of God, Christ, the Spirit, the cross, redemption, salvation, or eternal life, I would tell them that the true God is a loving and lovable God. I would go on to tell them the story of how God sent His Son, Jesus Christ, to accomplish redemption for us by dying on the cross. I would continue by telling them how wonderful Christ is. I would want them to know about His death on the cross and how He shed His blood so that we might be forgiven. I would tell them that through Christ's death and resurrection, the divine life within Him has been released. I would also tell them that now Christ, the living One, is the life-giving Spirit who is waiting to be received. Those who hear such a gospel message would spontaneously have the hearing of faith. The word that I would preach would be a word of grace. But once they have heard such a word, in their experience it would become the faith by which they believe.

When people hear of the grace of God in the preaching of the gospel, something rises up within them to appreciate what they have heard. The grace presented to them becomes in them the faith by which they believe. Spontaneously they begin to appreciate God, Christ, and the Spirit. They appreciate what Christ has done in accomplishing redemption. This appreciation is faith. Faith comes when they begin to appreciate what they hear in the gospel.

THE OBJECTIVE AND SUBJECTIVE
ASPECTS OF FAITH

Concerning faith there are two aspects, the objective aspect and the subjective aspect. Objectively faith is what we believe. Subjectively faith is our believing. Therefore, faith denotes both the act of believing and that in which we believe. Regarding the act of believing, faith is subjective, but regarding what we believe, faith is objective. As we hear about those things in which we are to believe, faith is produced within us. The more we hear about these good things, the more we appreciate them. Spontaneously this appreciation issues in our believing in those very things about which we have heard. Therefore, faith is both objective and subjective.

In 1:23 we are told that Paul, who once persecuted the believers in Christ, now preached "the faith which formerly he ravaged." Faith here and in 3:2, 5, 7, 9, 23, 25, and 6:10 implies our believing in Christ, taking His Person and His redemptive work as the object of our faith. This, replacing the law, by which God dealt with people in the Old Testament, becomes the principle of God's dealing with people in the New Testament. This faith characterizes the believers in Christ and distinguishes them from the keepers of law. This is the main emphasis of this book.

The subjective aspect of faith implies at least eight

items. First, faith involves hearing. Without the hearing of the word, there can be no faith. Faith comes from hearing. The word we hear includes God, Christ, the Spirit, the cross, redemption, salvation, forgiveness, and eternal life. It also includes the fact that God has been processed to become the all-inclusive life-giving Spirit. According to the New Testament, the gospel tells us of all these matters. When the gospel is preached in a proper way, those who hear it will be stirred up and filled with appreciation. Their hearing of the word of the gospel is the beginning of their believing. The reason Christians are lacking in faith is that their hearing is poor. If they heard a living message on how the Triune God has been processed to become the all-inclusive life-giving Spirit, no doubt this hearing would produce faith in them.

Second, faith also implies appreciation. After hearing the word of the gospel, a sense of appreciation spontaneously rises up in those who hear. This is true not only of those hearing the gospel for the first time, but for all believers in Christ. Whenever we hear the word in a proper way, this hearing awakens more appreciation for the Lord.

This appreciation is followed by calling, the third item implied in the subjective aspect of faith. All those who appreciate the Lord Jesus will spontaneously call on His name. If our gospel preaching is cold, dull, and dead, it will be necessary to persuade people to pray and call on the Lord's name. But if our preaching is precious, rich, living, inspiring, and stirring, there will be no need to persuade people. Rather, they will spontaneously call, "O Lord Jesus." Perhaps instead of calling on Him in this way, they will utter some word of appreciation for the Lord. Perhaps they will say, "Oh, how good the Lord Jesus is!"

Fourth, faith implies receiving. By appreciating the Lord Jesus and calling on Him, we spontaneously receive Him.

With receiving, we have the fifth aspect, that of accepting. It is possible to receive something without accepting it. Faith involves both receiving and accepting. Those who hear the gospel and appreciate the Lord Jesus automatically accept Him as well as receive Him.

Sixth, faith includes becoming joined to the Lord Jesus. By receiving and accepting Him, we are joined to Him.

Then, as the seventh and eighth items, we partake of Him and enjoy Him. Faith partakes of and enjoys what it receives and accepts.

In the preaching of the gospel, people hear of God's grace. Then they appreciate it and call upon the Lord. They go on to receive, accept, join, partake of, and enjoy this grace, which is the Triune God processed to be everything to us. This is faith.

THE HEARING OF FAITH
IN THE MEETINGS OF THE CHURCH

Faith was not to be found in the Old Testament; it came with Jesus Christ. When Christ came, grace came, and faith came also. Faith has come to replace law. Therefore, as believers in Christ, we are hearers, not workers. In the church meetings we gather together for the hearing of faith. Those who do not attend the meetings cut themselves off from opportunities for the hearing of faith. If we are cut off from the hearing, we are also cut off from the supply.

Do not stay away from the meetings because you think you will simply hear the same things over and over again. We need to eat breakfast every morning even though we may eat the same thing almost every day. If we refuse to eat because the food is the same, we shall not receive our necessary supply of food. In the same principle, we need to attend the church meetings in order to receive God's supply. We can testify that it makes a great difference whether or not we come to the meetings for the hearing of faith. Time and time again, we may hear of Christ and the church, of Christ's death and resurrection, and of how Christ has been processed to become the life-giving Spirit. But each time we hear these things, we receive the supply of the Spirit. Therefore, a proper Christian meeting is a hearing meeting, a meeting for the hearing of faith.

Those who speak in the church meetings should also be hearers, for they also hear the very things they are speaking. Those of us who speak in the church can testify that the more we speak, the more we hear. A proper speaker speaks first to himself and then to others. If you do not speak to yourself first, your speaking is not genuine. If we are genuine speakers, we should be the first to enjoy our speaking.

Meeting by meeting we come together for the hearing of faith. This faith is the appreciation, receiving, and accepting of God's grace. Through faith we are joined to God's grace, we partake of God's grace, and we enjoy God's grace. As we have pointed out again and again, this grace is the Triune God processed to become our enjoyment and everything to us.

GOD'S INTENTION IN HIS ECONOMY

How wrong the Galatian believers were to turn back to the law! God does not want us to be workers of law; He wants us to be hearers of His grace. As we hear His grace, grace spontaneously becomes our faith. Before faith came, God used the law to keep us, hold us, and retain us. But now that faith has come, we no longer need the law. With the law there is no enjoyment, no grace. But with faith there is an abundance of enjoyment, for faith is related to grace. Today we experience the hearing of faith. By this hearing of faith we continually receive the supply of the all-inclusive Spirit.

According to the revelation in the book of Galatians, God's New Testament economy is not that we strive in the flesh to keep the law. In this matter the Judaizers had altogether missed the mark. No genuine believers in Christ should be distracted by such folly. In His New Testament economy God intends to make us hearers of faith. This faith is the reflection of the Triune God processed to become our all-inclusive grace. God desires that we become those who continually hear the faith which reflects His grace. Grace is nothing less than the Triune God — the Father, the Son, and the Spirit — to be our life and our everything so that we may enjoy Him in a full way. Through this enjoyment we become one with Him. We become a universal and eternal entity to express His marvelous divinity. This is the revelation contained in the depths of this book.

LIFE-STUDY OF GALATIANS

THE SPIRIT — THE BLESSING OF THE GOSPEL

Scripture Reading: Gal. 3:5, 8-9, 14; Eph. 1:13; Acts 2:33, 39; John 7:39; 1 Cor. 15:45b; 2 Cor. 3:17; Phil. 1:19

THE CONTRAST BETWEEN FAITH AND LAW

In chapter three there is a strong contrast between faith and law. Law was the basis for the relationship between man and God in the Old Testament, whereas faith is the principle by which people contact God in the New Testament. The Old Testament was a dispensation of law, whereas the New Testament is a dispensation of faith. As the basis for the relationship between man and God, the law requires that man use his own effort to fulfill the law's requirements in order to please God. The law is not related to God intrinsically. Rather, it stands apart from God and places demands upon man that must be fulfilled if man is to please God. According to the principle of faith, man is not required to strive in his flesh to please God. Instead, man is to hear how God desires to be everything to him. God has planned to bless us. For our sake, He became incarnated, lived on earth, and died to accomplish redemption. He has been resurrected from among the dead and has become the life-giving Spirit. Now He is calling people to receive Him. He is eagerly expecting to come into people and to be their life and their everything so that they may be one with Him. This is the hearing of faith.

In this hearing of faith, we hear all the well-speaking of God, all His blessing. Faith involves the hearing concerning all the good things of God toward us. Through this hearing an appreciation for the Lord Jesus is awakened within us. Out of our appreciation for the Lord, we spon-

taneously call on His name. In this way we receive Him,
accept Him, and join ourselves to Him. Then we go on to
partake of Him and enjoy Him. All this is related to faith.
Law requires man to work, but faith receives all that God
is, all that God has planned and purposed, all that God has
accomplished, all that God has obtained and attained, and
all that God intends to impart into us. With law, there are
demands. But with faith there are no demands; there is
only the receiving of the processed Triune God. By receiving the Triune God, we also receive redemption, salvation,
forgiveness, eternal life, and all the heavenly, divine, and
spiritual things. What a contrast between law and faith!
Surely it is foolish to turn from faith and go back to the
law.

TWELVE CRUCIAL SUBJECTS

We have pointed out that Galatians 3 is a very difficult
chapter, one of the most difficult chapters in the New
Testament. In this chapter Paul seems to go from one subject to another. Many read this chapter without having any
idea what Paul is talking about. It seems that the points
covered are not related to one another. The way to understand this chapter is not to go verse by verse. Rather, it is
to concentrate on the main points. In this chapter Paul
covers at least twelve major subjects: Christ crucified;
Christ and the Spirit; the hearing of faith versus works of
law; the Spirit as the blessing of the gospel; the Spirit versus the flesh; the gospel preached to Abraham; the promise
versus the law; faith replacing law; the seed of Abraham
and the sons of Abraham; baptized into Christ; putting on
Christ; and all one in Christ. These are the crucial points
in this chapter. If we spend time to consider them and to
dwell on them in prayer, we shall be greatly helped in
understanding this chapter.

Having covered the subjects of Christ crucified, Christ
and the Spirit, and the hearing of faith versus works of law,
we come in this message to the Spirit as the blessing of the
gospel. During the years I have been a Christian, I have

heard that many things are the blessing of the gospel: salvation, redemption, forgiveness, eternal life. In Christianity people are often told that being able to go to heaven and to live in a mansion is a great blessing related to the gospel. Have you ever heard that the blessing of the gospel is the Spirit?

THE PROCESSED TRIUNE GOD

In the Bible, where words are always used economically, *the* Spirit has a particular meaning, somewhat different from the Holy Spirit. In Galatians Paul speaks not of the Holy Spirit, but of *the* Spirit. The total blessing of the gospel is not salvation, redemption, forgiveness, life, or going to heaven — it is the Spirit. The Spirit denotes the Triune God — the Father, the Son, and the Spirit — who has been processed through incarnation, human living, crucifixion, resurrection, and ascension. Only after He had entered into resurrection did the Lord Jesus command His disciples to baptize people into the name of the Father, of the Son, and of the Holy Spirit. The reason for this is that prior to the resurrection of Christ, the Triune God had not been fully processed. In the words of John 7:39, the Spirit was "not yet," even though the Holy Spirit was already in existence, as indicated by the record of Matthew 1 and Luke 1. The New Testament tells us clearly that the Holy Spirit was involved in the conception of the Lord Jesus in the womb of the virgin Mary. But *the* Spirit as the all-inclusive life-giving Spirit was "not yet" until the resurrection of Christ. John 7:39 tells us that the Spirit was not yet because Jesus was not yet glorified. The Lord was glorified in His resurrection (Luke 24:26). Therefore, after His glorification by resurrection, *the* Spirit was in existence.

From the Gospels we proceed to the Acts and to the Epistles. Paul's ministry was a completing ministry. In Colossians 1:25 he says that he became a minister according to the stewardship of God to complete the word of God. Hence, the completion of God's word is found neither in the Gospels, nor in the Acts, but in the Epistles of Paul.

In particular, the divine revelation is completed in four books: Galatians, Ephesians, Philippians, and Colossians. In Paul's Epistles the Spirit is revealed in a full way. We do not have such a revelation of the Spirit in the Gospels or in the Acts. The Spirit as revealed in Paul's writings is the Father, the Son, and the Spirit processed to become the all-inclusive life-giving Spirit. This Spirit enters into the believers to be their life and everything to them. Such a Spirit is the total blessing of the gospel. As the blessing of the gospel, the Spirit includes forgiveness, redemption, salvation, reconciliation, justification, eternal life, the divine nature, the uplifted and resurrected human nature, and the very Triune God Himself.

THE BLESSING OF ABRAHAM

Galatians 3:13 and 14 say, "Christ has redeemed us out of the curse of the law, having become a curse on our behalf; because it is written, Cursed is every one hanging on a tree, in order that the blessing of Abraham might come to the nations in Jesus Christ, that we might receive the promise of the Spirit through faith." Because it combines the promise of the Spirit with the blessing of Abraham, verse 14 is extremely important. The blessing of Abraham is the blessing promised by God to Abraham (Gen. 12:3) for all the nations of the earth. This promise was fulfilled, and this blessing has come to the nations in Christ through His redemption by the cross. The context of verse 14 indicates that the Spirit is the blessing which God promised to Abraham for all the nations and which has been received by the believers through faith in Christ. The Spirit is the compound Spirit and actually is God Himself processed in His Trinity through incarnation, crucifixion, resurrection, ascension, and descension, for us to receive as our life and our everything. This is the focus of the gospel of God.

The physical aspect of the blessing God promised to Abraham was the good land (Gen. 12:7; 13:15; 17:8; 26:3-4), which was a type of the all-inclusive Christ (Col. 1:12).

Since Christ is eventually realized as the all-inclusive life-giving Spirit (1 Cor. 15:45; 2 Cor. 3:17), the blessing of the promised Spirit corresponds to the blessing of the promised land. Actually, the Spirit as the realization of Christ in our experience is the good land as the source of God's bountiful supply for us to enjoy.

If we read the book of Genesis, we shall see that the focal point of God's promise to Abraham was that Abraham's seed would inherit the land. According to Galatians 3, Christ is this seed, the unique seed. Furthermore, as we have often pointed out, the good land is a full type of the all-inclusive Christ. On the one hand, the seed is Christ; on the other hand, the land is a type of Christ. The blessing of Abraham is altogether related to Christ. Christ is the focus of the promised blessing.

RECEIVING THE SPIRIT AS THE BLESSING

However, verse 14 does not say that in receiving the blessing of Abraham we receive Christ. Instead, this verse tells us that we receive the Spirit. Surely this indicates that the Spirit here is the blessing of Abraham.

What kind of Spirit could be the blessing God promised to Abraham? What Spirit would be the all-inclusive blessing, which is Christ as the seed and as the land? It must be *the* Spirit, the all-inclusive life-giving Spirit. First Corinthians 15:45 says that the last Adam became a life-giving Spirit, and 2 Corinthians 3:17 declares that now the Lord is the Spirit. In 2 Corinthians 3:17 the King James Version says "that Spirit." This rendering is not accurate, for the Greek word uses the definite article. Hence, the proper rendering is "the Spirit," referring to the Spirit who was "not yet" until Christ had been glorified.

At the time of the Lord's incarnation, the Holy Spirit began to have the element of humanity as well as divinity. From that time, the Holy Spirit was compounded with the Lord's human living, crucifixion, and resurrection and became the Spirit, the all-inclusive Spirit compounded with divinity, humanity, and the Lord's human living, death, and resurrection. All that God has purposed and planned and all that He has accomplished through incarnation, human living, crucifixion, and resurrection is included in *the* Spirit. Hence, *the* Spirit is all-inclusive, the Triune God processed to be everything to us. This Spirit is the blessing of the gospel.

RECEIVING THE SPIRIT BY FAITH

We have received this Spirit by faith. When we began to appreciate the Lord Jesus and believe in Him, we received the Spirit. In this receiving of the Spirit, the manifestation of gifts or the speaking in tongues had no place, for we received the Spirit by the hearing of faith.

A TESTIMONY TO THE PROPER EXPERIENCE
OF THE INNER LIFE

Let me tell you something of my own history. I was born into organized Christianity. After I was saved, I came to love the Bible. During my years with the Brethren, I acquired a considerable amount of Bible knowledge. Eventually, I met Brother Nee, one who knew both the inner life and the church. He helped me to experience the inner life and also the church life. Then in 1936, along with others, I began to pursue the so-called Pentecostal experiences, in particular, the experience of speaking in tongues. For a period of time, I was bold and strong in this matter. However, I came to realize that nothing can compare with the experience of the inner life in the church, and I gave up my involvement with the Pentecostal things. I spontaneously dropped those things in favor of enjoying the inner life in the church life. We did not receive any benefit from the Pentecostal things. On the contrary, those things only caused problems.

In 1943 the church in my home town, Chefoo, was carried away from the proper inner life to the excesses of the Pentecostal things. I was ill at the time, and the leading ones did not know how to handle the situation. We realized that this problem was related to the power of darkness and that the only way to deal with it was to pray. A while later, a sister in the church died of tuberculosis. Immediately, a sister who took the lead among those who spoke in tongues prophesied that the deceased sister would be raised from the dead at noon the following day. This particular sister went on to tell the husband of the sister who had died that there was no need for him to make funeral arrangements since his wife would be raised from the dead. The next day hundreds of people gathered together, waiting for this miracle to take place. They waited until twelve noon, but nothing happened. Finally, about three o'clock in the afternoon, one of the elders told the people that they should pay no further attention to the nonsensical prophecy which had been given. He further advised the husband of the deceased sister to make the necessary arrangements for the funeral. The crowd was dispersed, and everyone went home, disappointed and dejected. This one incident caused the church to come back to the proper experience of the inner life, and to turn away from the Pentecostal things.

As the all-inclusive life-giving Spirit, the processed Triune God inspires His servants to preach the good word of the gospel. As people listen to this well-speaking, spontaneously an appreciation for the Lord Jesus is stirred up within them. They also appreciate Christ's redemption, eternal life, and the precious forgiveness of sins. Out of their appreciation they call on the Lord and thereby receive the Spirit as the full blessing of the gospel of God. The experience and the expression may differ, but we all are the same in having received the Spirit. No matter how we were brought to the Lord, we all have received the Spirit as the blessing of the gospel through the hearing faith.

THE DEVELOPMENT OF THE ORGANIC UNION

In God's New Testament economy, the principle of the hearing of faith replaces the law. By faith we are brought into an organic union with the Triune God. If we had not been frustrated by religion with its teachings, this organic union would have been fully developed by now. Today in His recovery the Lord is developing this organic union, and He will cause it to be developed to the uttermost. The more this union is developed, the more we enjoy the total blessing of the gospel.

THE COMPOUND SPIRIT

The Spirit we have received as the blessing of the gospel is the all-inclusive, compound Spirit typified by the compound ointment in Exodus 30:23-25. The compounding of the spices with the olive oil to produce the ointment typifies the compounding of Christ's humanity, death, and resurrection with the Spirit of God to produce the all-inclusive Spirit. This Spirit is the bountiful supply to the believers in God's New Testament economy (Gal. 3:5; Phil. 1:19). By faith we have received this Spirit as the blessing of the gospel promised to Abraham by God. As the processed Triune God, the Spirit is the full realization of the all-inclusive Christ as the good land. This is the Spirit as the total blessing of the gospel.

LIFE-STUDY OF GALATIANS

MESSAGE SIXTEEN

THE SPIRIT VERSUS THE FLESH

Scripture Reading: Gal. 3:2-3, 5, 14; 5:16-19; 1:16; 2:16; 4:23, 29; 5:13, 22; 6:8, 12-13; 4:6; 5:5, 25

In this message we come to a very crucial subject: the Spirit versus the flesh. Because of the influence of our background in Christianity, our understanding of the terms Spirit and flesh in the New Testament is limited. Actually, these terms have a very broad significance. They are two of the most important expressions used in the New Testament.

DEFINITIONS OF THE FLESH AND THE SPIRIT

In 3:3 Paul asks the Galatian believers, "Having begun by the Spirit, are you now being perfected by the flesh?" The Spirit, who is the resurrected Christ, is of life. The flesh, which is our fallen man, is of sin and death. We should not begin by the Spirit and attempt to be perfected by the flesh. Those of us who have begun by the Spirit should be perfected by the Spirit and have nothing to do with the flesh. In 2:20 the contrast is between Christ and "I"; here the contrast is between the Spirit and the flesh. This indicates that the Spirit is Christ and the flesh is "I" in our experience. From chapter three to the end of the Epistle, the Spirit is Christ in our life experience. In revelation it is Christ; in experience it is the Spirit.

The flesh is condemned and repudiated throughout this entire book (1:16; 2:16; 3:3; 4:23, 29; 5:13, 16-17, 19; 6:8, 12-13), and from chapter three, every chapter gives a contrast between the flesh and the Spirit (3:3; 4:29; 5:16-17, 19, 22; 6:8). The flesh is the uttermost expression of the fallen tripartite man, and the Spirit is the ultimate realization of the processed Triune God. The flesh inclines to keep the law and is tested by the law. The Spirit is received and enjoyed by faith. God's economy delivers us from the flesh to the Spirit that we may participate in the blessing of the riches of the Triune God. This cannot take place by the flesh keeping the law, but takes place by the Spirit being received by faith and experienced through faith.

In the book of Galatians, the flesh does not refer merely to man's fallen and corrupted body. Rather, it refers to the totality of man's fallen being. The flesh is therefore the uttermost expression of the fallen tripartite man. Hence, the flesh in this sense includes man's body, soul, and spirit. If you consider the works of the flesh listed in 5:19-21, you will find that some, such as fornication, uncleanness, sensuality, and drunkenness, are related to the lust of the corrupted body; others, such as enmities, strife, angers, and divisions, are related to the fallen soul; and still others, idolatry and sorcery, are related to the deadened spirit. This proves that the three parts of our fallen being are involved with the evil flesh. Therefore, in Galatians the flesh denotes the whole of man's fallen being. The flesh is not just a part of man's fallen being; it includes the totality of the fallen tripartite man.

According to the revelation in the New Testament, the Spirit is the ultimate realization of the processed Triune God. God is the Spirit, and fallen man is the flesh. God is the processed Triune God, and the flesh is the fallen tripartite man. Have you ever realized that man today is the fallen tripartite man and that God is the processed Triune God? The fallen tripartite man is the flesh, and the processed Triune God is the Spirit. Just as the flesh in Galatians refers not only to the corrupted and lustful body, but to the totality of fallen man, so the Spirit refers not only to the third Person of the Triune God, but to the Triune God who has been processed through incarnation, human living, crucifixion, resurrection, and ascension. The flesh refers to our entire fallen being, and the Spirit, to the entire Triune God, to the Father, the Son, and the Spirit. Having

been processed through incarnation, human living, crucifixion, resurrection, and ascension, the Triune God is
today the Spirit. When we read of the flesh in the New Testament, we need to realize that it denotes the totality of
man's fallen being. In the same principle, when we read
of the Spirit in the Epistles of Paul, we need to understand that the Spirit denotes the Triune God — the Father,
the Son, and the Spirit — processed to become the all-
inclusive life-imparting Spirit.

SATAN'S MISUSE OF THE LAW

God's economy is to dispense Himself as the processed
Triune God into our being to be our life and our everything, to make Himself one with us and us one with Him so
that we may express Him in a corporate way for eternity.
However, in the attempt to frustrate God's economy,
Satan, the enemy of God, uses the law, which was
given by God to serve His purpose temporarily, to keep
God's chosen people from His economy and to distract
them from it. If we look at the book of Galatians from this
point of view, we shall find that it is not difficult to understand. As we read this Epistle, we need to see that God's
economy is to impart Himself as the all-inclusive life-
giving Spirit into us to produce an organic union between
us and the Triune God so that we may express Him in a
corporate way. But Satan utilizes the law given by God in
order to distract God's people from His economy and to
hinder the fulfillment of God's economy.

It is important to understand clearly what it means for
the law to be misused. The law is misused when it is used
to stir up fallen man's desire to uplift himself by keeping
the law in order to have a self-made righteousness. The
Judaizers misused the law in this way to distract the
believers from God's economy. What we see in the book of
Galatians is this misuse of the God-given law. The law
given by God was misused by Satan to keep God's chosen
people from God's economy.

THE WAY OF FAITH

In a foregoing message we have pointed out that the works of law are contrary to the hearing of faith. Faith is the way for God's people to apprehend, comprehend, grasp, enjoy, and participate in all that God is to His people through His having been processed to become the Spirit. According to Galatians, the law has been replaced by faith. In our experience, the law should be over, and faith should be prevailing.

Just as the law and the flesh go together, so faith and the Spirit go together. Whenever we try to keep the law, we are immediately in the flesh. But when we take the way of faith to hear, appreciate, call upon, receive, accept, join, partake of, and enjoy, we spontaneously experience the Spirit. This can be confirmed by our experience. Whenever we strive to keep the law, we are in the flesh, in the fallen tripartite man. But whenever we take the way of faith, we are in our spirit enjoying the Spirit. Here, in the way of faith, we enjoy the Spirit as the processed Triune God. Furthermore, the way of faith causes the organic union between the processed God and regenerated man to be developed and cultivated. God intends that this organic union be developed to the uttermost.

HOW SATAN FRUSTRATES THE DEVELOPMENT
OF THE ORGANIC UNION

However, I am burdened to point out that in his subtlety, Satan has frustrated the cultivation and development of this organic union. He has done this through the use of three isms: Catholicism, Protestantism, and Pentecostalism. These three isms in today's Christianity have been utilized by Satan to hinder God's economy by frustrating the development of the organic union between the regenerated man and the processed Triune God. Suppose that in this country these three isms did not exist, and there was only the Lord's recovery. If this were the situation, surely the organic union between us and God would become highly developed in a short period of time. However, it is a fact that this organic union has been frustrated. It has been frustrated not mainly by Judaism, Islam, or Buddhism, but by Catholicism, Protestantism, and Pentecostalism. Just as Satan used Judaism in ancient times, so he uses these isms today to keep God's people from the proper development of their organic union with the Triune God.

The principle Satan follows in doing this is to take something given by God and to cause it to be used in a wrong way. This principle can be seen, for instance, in Catholicism, where certain God-given things can be found. Many genuine believers in Catholicism have been bewitched by Satan's use of these God-given things. Because certain things of God can be found in the Catholic Church, many will rise up to vindicate it, arguing that there is certainly something of God to be found there. Let us remember the Lord's prophecy in Matthew 13:33 concerning the Catholic Church: "Another parable He spoke to them: The kingdom of the heavens is like leaven, which a woman took and hid in three measures of meal until the whole was leavened." Like the woman in this parable, the Catholic Church has mixed leaven with fine flour. It has blended satanic things with the things given by God. Therefore, what we find in Catholicism is a mixture of Satanic things and God-given things. In Revelation 17 the Catholic Church is presented as a woman with a golden cup full of abominations. This is the actual situation of Catholicism.

In the same principle, we cannot deny that there is something of God in Protestantism. Some things given by God are found there. However, Satan utilizes these things to frustrate God's economy and to hinder the development of the organic union. Most of the genuine believers in the Protestant denominations have never even heard of this organic union. Many do not even know that Christ lives in them. People may be brought to the Lord through Catholicism or Protestantism. But after they have been brought to Him, they are hindered from going on to experience Him.

Through the gospel preaching in Protestantism, many sinners have been saved. Nevertheless, after they were saved and became believers, they were kept from experiencing Christ by the very denominations through which they were saved.

The third ism, Pentecostalism, is more subtle than Catholicism and Protestantism. After more than fifty years of study and experience, I can testify that nothing is more subtle in hindering God's people from experiencing Christ than today's Pentecostalism. For a number of years, we in the Lord's recovery in China were under the influence of the Pentecostal things. Through our experience we can testify that our involvement with Pentecostalism was more of a loss than a gain.

The greatest damage of Pentecostalism is that it makes it difficult for believers to appreciate the inward organic union with the Triune God. The emphasis in Pentecostalism is on outward manifestations. It is difficult for those who emphasize such things to calm down and know the Spirit in their regenerated spirit and to follow the inner anointing. Many in Pentecostalism neither know nor care that they have a regenerated spirit. Rather, they care mainly for the manifestation of the so-called gifts. They are interested in speaking in tongues, healing, and miracles, not in the development and cultivation of the organic union with the Triune God.

In 1963 I was invited to speak to a certain Pentecostal group. After one of the meetings, the leader of this group and his wife tried to get a particular Chinese brother to speak in tongues. The wife told him not to speak either English or Chinese, but any other words which came to mind. The brother realized that in order to get out of that situation he had to say something. Remembering a few words in the Malay language he happened to know, he uttered some nonsensical expression in that language. Immediately the leader of this Pentecostal group and his wife clapped their hands and rejoiced that this brother had spoken in tongues. The next day I pointed out to that couple what had actually happened and went on to question them about this practice.

Furthermore, in one of the meetings of this same Pentecostal group, a woman gave a short word in tongues. Then a young man gave a long interpretation of that word. Later the leader of the group admitted that the interpretation given by the young man was not genuine. I then asked him why he engaged in these practices when we have such a rich Christ to minister to others. He had nothing to say in response to my question. Much later the young man who had given that interpretation denied that what he spoke was intended to be the interpretation of that woman's message in tongues. I reminded him that he had clearly indicated to all present that he was giving an interpretation. I went on to say, "There is no need for us to do these things. I definitely believe that you love the Lord. Why don't you simply preach the truth and minister the riches of Christ to others?"

The claim has even been made in some Pentecostal groups that in their meetings people's teeth have been filled with gold miraculously. I absolutely do not believe such reports. Why would God not restore the teeth instead of filling them with gold? That would be more in agreement with the principle in the Bible. Furthermore, if such miracles had actually taken place, newsmen would learn of them and publicize them.

Another case concerns the leader in a Pentecostal group who claimed that he had been given the ability to speak Chinese. One day he uttered certain peculiar sounds, believing that he was speaking the Chinese language. I and another Chinese-speaking brother pointed out that we could not understand a word he said, even though I spoke Mandarin, the other brother spoke Cantonese, and we both had understanding of other Chinese dialects. However, this Pentecostal leader proceeded to utter some different sounds. We also had to tell him that we could not recognize them as words in the Chinese language. When this brother heard this, he was disappointed. In his self-deception he had the assurance that he was able to speak Chinese. But the Chinese he spoke was a self-made language. Such incidents are common in today's Pentecostalism.

A certain charismatic magazine printed an article in which the writer said that he had contacted two hundred people who claimed to speak in tongues. Without exception, all of these two hundred doubted that the tongue spoken was genuine. However, the writer encouraged them all to go on speaking in tongues regardless of their doubts about the genuineness of what they were uttering. We read this article publicly in the training in 1963. Then I asked the trainees if Peter and the others on the day of Pentecost had any doubt whether the tongues spoken by them were genuine. Certainly Peter and the others had no such doubts. However, these two hundred tongues-speakers had doubts because the tongues they spoke were not genuine.

In 1963 and 1964 there were newspaper reports about some Pentecostal prophecies that an earthquake would strike the city of Los Angeles and that the city would fall into the ocean. However, the date of the predicted earthquake passed, and nothing happened. Certainly this lack of fulfillment is sufficient to prove that this prophecy was a falsehood.

I would like to cite another example from our experience in the Far East. After we had moved to Taiwan and had begun the work there, I pointed out to the saints that, according to our experience on the mainland, it was best that we leave Christianity alone. I also advised them not to become involved with Pentecostal things. Instead, I encouraged them simply to preach the gospel to unbelievers. For years we preached the gospel in an aggressive way, flooding the cities with tracts and posters. After six years, our number increased from less than five hundred to more than twenty thousand. During the early 1960s, while I was away from Taiwan, a certain Pentecostal woman minister became quite prevailing in Malaysia and exerted a considerable influence over some saints in the Lord's recovery. She even seized control of a small church in Malaysia. However, one elderly brother and three young people refused to go along with this situation, for they were clear concerning the truth. In 1965 this lady preacher planned to hold a conference in Taiwan, especially for those in the local churches. She intended to take over all the churches on the island of Taiwan. Although I had no knowledge of this situation, I became burdened to visit Taiwan in September 1965, the very month this conference was scheduled. When I arrived, I learned for the first time of this conference. This woman, who was noted for saying that it was not necessary for tongues-speaking to be a real dialect or language, suddenly developed cancer of the tongue and was not able to go to Taiwan for the conference. Prophecies were given that a world-wide revival would begin from Taiwan in 1966 and that she would be healed. However, there was no revival, and she died. After her death, a prophecy was made and put in writing that she would be resurrected. But this so-called prophecy was not fulfilled.

WALKING ACCORDING TO THE SPIRIT
IN OUR SPIRIT

Because of all that I have learned and experienced, sometimes with much suffering, I have come to realize that along with Catholicism and Protestantism, Pentecostalism is a frustration to God's economy. It is a great hindrance to the development of the organic union between us and the Triune God. According to Paul's Epistles, the Triune God has been processed to become the all-inclusive life-giving Spirit. When this Spirit comes into man's spirit, an organic union is created. Now that we are organically united to the Triune God, we can live by Him in our spirit.

In 1 Corinthians Paul was dealing with the misuse of tongues-speaking. In chapter seven of this book we find an excellent example of living according to the organic union. In verse 25 Paul says, "Now concerning virgins I have no commandment of the Lord: yet I give my judgment, as one that hath obtained mercy of the Lord to be faithful." After presenting his opinion on the matter, Paul concludes by saying, "I think also that I have the Spirit of God" (v. 40). Here we see the New Testament way, the way of incarnation. According to this way, there is the mingling of divinity with humanity. God does not act alone, and man does not act alone. Rather, God acts in oneness with His saved people, for an organic union has taken place between the processed Triune God and those who have been regenerated. All that we say and do should issue from this union, this mingling of God and man. This is very different from the practice of today's Pentecostalism, which in its so-called prophecies follows the Old Testament way of saying, "Thus saith the Lord." In the New Testament, however, we do not read of "Thus saith the Lord"; instead we read of what Paul says or of what Peter and John say. According to 1 Corinthians 7, even though Paul had no commandment from the Lord regarding virgins, he could still speak a word in which the Spirit of God was expressed. This is the New Testament way. We need to follow this way to develop the organic union between the processed God and regenerated man.

We have pointed out emphatically that in Galatians the Spirit denotes the processed Triune God and that the flesh denotes the totality of the fallen tripartite man. If we see this contrast, we shall not want to live in ourselves, apart from God. Anything we do independently of the Lord is of the flesh. It is crucial that we realize that we have been joined organically to the Triune God. He and we, we and He, are mingled together as one. Such an organic union has taken place in our spirit. Therefore, we should walk according to the Spirit in our spirit. This is God's New Testament economy, the way in which His eternal purpose is carried out.

LIFE-STUDY OF GALATIANS

MESSAGE SEVENTEEN

THE GOSPEL PREACHED TO ABRAHAM

Scripture Reading: Gal. 3:6-11, 14, 16-17; Gen. 12:7; Col. 1:12b; Eph. 3:6, 9, 11

When I first learned that long before Christ came the gospel was preached to Abraham, I was greatly surprised. Galatians 3:8 says, "And the Scripture, foreseeing that God would justify the nations by faith, preached the gospel beforehand to Abraham: In you all the nations shall be blessed." According to Genesis 12:3, in Abraham all the nations would be blessed. In Genesis 12:7 the Lord went on to say to Abraham, "Unto thy seed will I give this land." There are two main aspects of God's word to Abraham in Genesis 12: the first is that in him all nations would be blessed; the second is that the land would be given to Abraham's seed. In Christ, Abraham's unique seed, the nations would be blessed. Furthermore, to this unique seed the land would be given. This was God's word to Abraham.

In Galatians 3:16 Paul refers to God's word to Abraham as a promise: "To Abraham were the promises spoken and to his seed." Then in verse 17 Paul goes on to speak of a covenant ratified beforehand by God. This indicates that the promise God gave to Abraham became a covenant, which is more firm than a promise. The word, the promise, and the covenant are the gospel which was preached to Abraham. The gospel is the covenant, the covenant is the promise, and the promise is the word spoken by God.

It is important to see the difference between these four terms. A word is common or ordinary, whereas a promise is much more specific. If you give a promise to someone, your word is not common; it is specific. You promise to do certain things for that person. The word God spoke to Abraham in Genesis 12 was not common; it was a specific word in which God promised Abraham that in him and in his seed the nations would be blessed. We have pointed out that in this chapter God also promised Abraham that his seed would possess the land. Because the word spoken to Abraham in Genesis 12 is very specific, it is a word of promise.

In Genesis 15 this promise became a covenant. Here God appeared to Abraham, and Abraham offered a sacrifice to Him. The sacrifice was divided, and God passed through it. This was a custom in ancient times by which two parties ratified a covenant. By walking through the sacrifice, these parties ratified a covenant in an official and proper manner. In this way the promise given in Genesis 12 was ratified as a covenant in Genesis 15. Then in Genesis 17 the covenant was confirmed by the sign of circumcision.

In Galatians 3 Paul says that the word spoken to Abraham, the word which became a covenant confirmed by circumcision, was the gospel preached to Abraham. In Galatians 3 we are given Paul's understanding and interpretation. Perhaps this interpretation came as a revelation to Paul during the years he was alone with the Lord. Paul came to see that what God had spoken to Abraham was not just a promise or merely a covenant ratified and confirmed, but that it was the very gospel. In this covenant, Paul learned, the main items of the new testament gospel were included. Thus, the covenant ratified with Abraham was a forerunner of the new covenant, of the new testament.

The new testament is a new covenant ratified by the sacrifice of the Lord Jesus. The Lord offered Himself up as a sacrifice to God. In a sense, God walked through the sacrifice offered to Him on the cross by Christ. This new covenant may be considered as either a repetition or a continuation of the covenant ratified with Abraham. The gospel we are preaching today is not merely a promise; it is also a covenant.

In message forty-one of the Life-study of Hebrews, we pointed out the difference between a covenant and a testament. A covenant refers to an agreement concerning things promised, but not yet accomplished. A testament denotes an agreement in which the promised items have been accomplished. When all the items of the promise are accomplished, the covenant becomes a testament. The modern term for testament is will. The new testament is the new will. A will is not an agreement in which the testator promises to do certain things for others. No, a will is a testament which says that the testator has already done certain things or given certain things to particular people. The gospel we preach is first a covenant. Ultimately, however, it is a testament. At the time of Abraham this gospel could not have been a testament. It could only have been a covenant in which God promised to bless all the nations in Abraham and to give the good land to Abraham's seed. Later, in Genesis 15, this promise became a ratified covenant. But for us the new covenant is a new testament because all the promised things have been accomplished by Christ. All the nations have been blessed in Christ, and the good land has been given to Abraham's seed. Therefore, what we receive today is not a new covenant; it is a new testament, a new will. This will is the gospel.

Paul received a marvelous understanding of spiritual things. Without the revelation given to him, we would not have the confidence to say that the covenant ratified with Abraham was the gospel preached to Abraham. But Paul boldly declares that the Scripture, foreseeing that God would justify the nations by faith, preached the gospel beforehand to Abraham (3:8). Apart from Paul's word in Galatians 3, we would not realize that God's word to Abraham was the gospel. Although the gospel is a matter of the new testament, it is important for us to realize that the new testament is a continuation or repetition of God's promise to Abraham.

I. THE GOSPEL BY FAITH
THROUGH MAN'S BELIEVING

In 3:6-9 we see that the gospel is by faith through man's believing. This gospel was altogether by faith, not by works of law. In Genesis 12, 15, and 17 Abraham had the hearing of faith. This hearing stirred up a sense of appreciation within him. We are told that Abraham believed God and that God reckoned his believing as righteousness (Gen. 15:6). The preaching of the gospel was received by Abraham through the hearing of faith.

II. NOT AS THE LAW BY WORKS
THROUGH MAN'S WORKING

The gospel is not as the law, which is by works through man's working. In 3:10 and 11 we see a contrast between the gospel by faith and the law by works. The one is through man's believing; the other, through man's working.

III. PREACHED BEFORE THE GIVING
OF THE LAW THROUGH MOSES

The gospel was preached not only before the accomplishing of redemption by Christ, but also before the giving of the law through Moses. In 3:17 Paul says, "And I say this, a covenant ratified beforehand by God, the law having come four hundred and thirty years after does not annul, so as to make the promise of none effect." God's promise to Abraham was given first. The law came four hundred thirty years later. The promise was permanent, but the law was temporary. The temporary law, which came later, cannot annul the permanent promise, which came first. The Galatians left the first and permanent promise and went back to the later and temporary law.

The four hundred thirty years mentioned in 3:17 are counted from the time God gave Abraham the promise in Genesis 12 to the time He gave the law through Moses in Exodus 20. This period was considered by God as the time of the children of Israel's dwelling in Egypt (Exo. 12:40-41). The four hundred years mentioned in Genesis 15:13 and Acts 7:6 are counted from the time Ishmael mocked Isaac in Genesis 21 to the time the children of Israel came out of Egyptian tyranny in Exodus 12. This is the period when Abraham's descendants suffered the persecution of the Gentiles.

Paul's intention was to show that the law given through Moses was not God's original intention, but something secondary and additional. Because the law is not like Sarah, the genuine wife, but like Hagar, the concubine, it does not have the proper position. It was given four hundred thirty years after the gospel was preached to Abraham. Since God does not change, how could He preach the gospel to Abraham and then, four hundred thirty years later, command the people to fulfill the law in order to satisfy Him? The law was given for the purpose of exposing God's chosen people and keeping them in His custody.

IV. AS A PROMISE GIVEN TO ABRAHAM

The gospel was preached to Abraham as the promise that in him all nations would be blessed. The word blessed in Genesis 12:3 is of great significance. Through Adam's fall, the human race was brought under the curse. But God promised Abraham that in him and because of him the nations, which had been brought under the curse, would be blessed. According to Galatians 3:13, the curse has been taken away. Christ has redeemed us out of the curse of the law so that the blessing of Abraham might come to the nations in Him. Christ died a substitutionary death on the cross to deliver us from the curse brought in by Adam. Now in Christ all the nations will be blessed. Hence, the blessing promised to Abraham comes to us through Christ's redemption. The curse has been taken away, and the blessing has come. All the nations have been blessed in Christ, Abraham's unique seed.

This blessing has the good land as the center. The good

land typifies the all-inclusive Christ realized by the all-inclusive life-giving Spirit to be the blessing of the gospel (Gen. 12:7; Col. 1:12b; Gal. 3:14). We have pointed out again and again that the good land is a complete type of the all-inclusive Christ. After His resurrection, Christ is realized as the all-inclusive life-giving Spirit. Ultimately, this all-inclusive life-giving Spirit is our good land. Since the Spirit in Galatians denotes the processed Triune God, we may say that the good land is the very processed Triune God. In the gospel what God gives us is nothing less than Himself.

To children, their mother is everything. As long as children have their mother, they are happy. Using this as an illustration of our relationship to the Triune God, we can say that the processed Triune God is the all-inclusive One who is everything to us and that this One is our good land. When the children of Israel entered into the good land, they had no lack. Therefore, this good land is a type of the processed Triune God who is realized in full as the all-inclusive Spirit indwelling our spirit. The good land today is in our spirit.

When the all-inclusive Spirit comes into our spirit, a certain transaction takes place. This transaction is what we call the organic union. In his *Word Studies in The New Testament,* M.R. Vincent, commenting on Matthew 28:19, says that "baptizing into the name of the Holy Trinity implies a spiritual and mystical union with Him." The Greek word for "into" in Matthew 28:19 indicates a union in life. Thus, baptism should not be a ritual; it should be the accomplishment of the organic union.

It is ridiculous to ask believers if they have received the Spirit. How could we have failed to receive the Spirit inasmuch as we have entered into an organic union with the Triune God? We have been grafted into Him. The process of grafting begins with appreciating the Lord, and it is accomplished by baptism. When you first heard the gospel, an appreciation for the Lord Jesus was awakened within you. Then you were willing to be baptized, at which time the organic union, the grafting, was accomplished. You were grafted into the Triune God. A sinner who believes in Jesus can then be baptized into the name of the Father, the Son, and the Spirit. The name denotes the Person. How marvelous that sinners can be baptized into the Triune God! The union accomplished through baptism is an intrinsic union, a union in life. If someone asks you if you have received the Holy Spirit, you may want to tell him that you have received the Triune God, the Father, the Son, and the Holy Spirit.

If we were to preach the gospel in a place where no one had heard the gospel before, those who heard our messages would immediately experience the organic union with the Triune God. Then we could easily help them to develop this union and not to live any longer by the self. To live by the organic union is to live by the Spirit, by the processed Triune God. There is no need for us to seek experiences such as speaking in tongues, for we can live by the Triune God in our spirit. In Taiwan we did not practice tongues-speaking, but within six years we increased from five hundred to twenty thousand. By contrast, many of those who emphasize the Pentecostal things have been fruitless. The organic union with the Triune God is much more powerful and prevailing than speaking in tongues. It is not necessary to practice tongues-speaking to have spiritual power. Through the organic union with the Triune God, I am energized and filled with power. The Lord's recovery has spread to five continents, not through speaking in tongues, but through the organic union. Praise the Lord that this organic union is in us all! I have the confidence that the recovery will continue to spread by means of this union. Again and again we need to come back to our spirit to experience the hearing of faith. The more hearing we have, the more appreciation there will be and also more calling, receiving, accepting, joining, partaking, and enjoying.

Galatians 3:8 says that the nations are justified by faith. In verse 11 Paul goes on to say, "Now that by law no one is justified before God is evident, because, The just by faith shall live." In verse 14 Paul points out that we receive the promise of the Spirit through faith. Faith in Christ brings us into the blessing God promised to Abraham, which is the promise of the Spirit. The believing ones are justified by faith, and they have life and live by faith. As justified ones, we live by the organic union and participate in the all-inclusive life-giving Spirit. This Spirit is the blessing of the gospel. What God promised to Abraham corresponds to what He accomplished by Christ. This accomplishment is the fulfillment of His promise to Abraham. Moreover, it is according to God's eternal purpose and His new testament economy (Eph. 3:6, 9, 11).

LIFE-STUDY OF GALATIANS

THE PROMISE VERSUS THE LAW

Scripture Reading: Gal. 3:2b, 3b, 6, 9-11, 13-14, 17, 21-25

The New Testament reveals that, in eternity past, God made a purpose, a plan. This purpose was to have a people chosen by Him to receive the sonship and thereby to become sons of God, with the Son of God as the Firstborn, and then to be formed into a corporate man to express God for eternity. This is a brief statement of God's eternal purpose. After conceiving this purpose, God accomplished the work of creation. The focal point of God's creation is man, because God's purpose is to have a people for His expression. We know from Genesis 1 that man was made in God's image and according to God's likeness. In other words, man was created with the potential to express God. At the time of creation, man had neither the divine life nor the divine nature. However, he was created with the capacity to receive God and to become one with Him.

THE FALL, THE CURSE, AND THE PROMISE

We know that after creation, man fell. On the one hand, the fall of Adam brought in sin and sins; on the other hand, Adam's fall brought in the curse. Hence, the man created by God in His own image and according to His likeness became involved with sin and came under the curse. The fact that mankind followed a downward course after Genesis 3 indicates that man is under a curse. We see this curse with Cain, the second generation of mankind. Because Cain's descendants were all under the curse, they fell lower and lower. Eventually, man fell to such a degree that, at Babel, he became divided and confused. There can be no doubt that fallen man is both involved with sin and under the curse.

In the midst of such a fallen situation, the God of glory appeared to Abraham (Acts 7:2). It is significant that the Bible does not say that the God of love appeared to Abraham, but says that the God of glory appeared to him. With Adam we have sin and the curse, but with Abraham we have God's promise. According to Genesis 12:3, God promised Abraham that in him all the nations would be blessed. The background of this promise was the curse upon mankind. Because mankind was under a curse, man's direction was downward. But God came in, called Abraham, and promised that in him the nations, mankind in a state of division and confusion, would be blessed. Certainly this was good news. It is no wonder, then, that Paul considered it the gospel.

However, the matter we are emphasizing here is the promise. In calling Abraham, God gave him a promise. In Galatians 3:17 Paul speaks of both a promise and a covenant. In this chapter he also tells us, in verse 8, that God's word to Abraham in Genesis 12:3 was the preaching of the gospel to Abraham. The speaking of that promise was the preaching of the gospel. Furthermore, the covenant ratified in Genesis 15 was the confirmation of the gospel.

In Genesis 12:3 the promise was only a promise, for it was still in need of fulfillment. In this chapter we are not told when, how, or where the promise would be fulfilled. Then in Genesis 15 the promise became a ratified covenant, and in Genesis 17 this covenant was confirmed by the sign of circumcision. However, even though the promise had been ratified as a covenant and confirmed, it still had not been fulfilled.

GOD DEALING WITH HIS PEOPLE
ACCORDING TO THE PROMISE

At the time God was ratifying the promise in Genesis 15, making it a covenant, a great darkness came upon

Abraham (v. 12). This darkness was an indication that before the promise would be fulfilled, God's people would undergo a time of darkness and suffer intensely. The Bible records that Abraham's descendants went into Egypt and spent at least four hundred years under Egyptian tyranny. These years were a long period of darkness. Then, after those four hundred years, God brought them out of the darkness of Egyptian tyranny. God did not deal with them according to the law, which had not yet been given, but He dealt with them according to the promise He made to Abraham, their forefather.

It is difficult to find a verse in the book of Exodus telling us that God's intention in bringing the children of Israel out of Egypt was to give them the law. However, it is clearly stated that God intended for them to hold a feast unto Him. Moses said to Pharaoh, "Thus saith the Lord God of Israel, Let my people go, that they may hold a feast unto me in the wilderness" (Exo. 5:1). No doubt, God also planned to reveal to them the pattern of His dwelling place.

Before Exodus 19, there seems to be no indication that God had any intention to give them the law. At the beginning of this chapter, God spoke very pleasant words to the people: "Ye have seen what I did unto the Egyptians, and how I bare you on eagles' wings, and brought you unto myself" (Exo. 19:4). The Lord went on to tell them that if they would obey His voice and keep His covenant, they would be a special treasure unto Him and become a kingdom of priests and a holy nation (vv. 5-6). God's word was very gracious. When the people heard what God had spoken, they answered, "All that the Lord hath spoken we will do" (v. 8). After this response of the people, the atmosphere around Mount Sinai changed. The cherishing atmosphere was replaced by a terrifying one. Frightened by this atmosphere, the children of Israel told Moses to be their representative to meet with God. In the midst of such a situation, the Ten Commandments were given. Therefore, with Adam we have the fall; with Abraham, the promise;

and with Moses, the law. Chapters twenty through twenty-three of Exodus are all related to the law.

But immediately following these chapters with their decrees and ordinances, we come to chapter twenty-four, where the situation around Mount Sinai is changed again. Moses, Aaron, Nadab, Abihu, and the seventy elders of Israel went up the mountain. In the words of Exodus 24:10, "they saw the God of Israel: and there was under his feet as it were a paved work of a sapphire stone, and as it were the body of heaven in his clearness." What a beautiful scene this was! It was in such a setting that God revealed to Moses the pattern of the tabernacle.

ACCORDING TO THE LAW
AND THROUGH THE TABERNACLE

After the law with its ordinances was given to the people, God dealt with the children of Israel according to the law through the tabernacle. The people did not contact God through the law, but they contacted Him through the tabernacle with the priesthood and the offerings. All these were the fulfillment, in type, of God's promise to Abraham. God dealt with the people according to the law through the tabernacle, the priesthood, and the offerings. Suppose an Israelite committed a sin. According to the Ten Commandments, he was to be cut off. But, instead of having him cut off, God fulfilled His promise to Abraham to bless all nations by blessing such a sinner through the altar. The one who committed the sin had to bring a sacrifice as a trespass offering. When this sacrifice was offered on the altar, the one who had sinned could be forgiven.

God used the law as a mirror to expose His people. But after the people were exposed, they could turn to the tabernacle, the priesthood, the altar, and the offerings. In type this was the fulfillment of the promise God made to Abraham. The book of Exodus is not actually a book of law; it is a book of the fulfillment of God's promise, a book of Christ, the cross, and the church. Yes, certain chapters are devoted to the law and its ordinances. But other chapters give the pattern of the tabernacle and describe the setting up of the tabernacle. As we have pointed out, it was in the midst of a clear atmosphere that the pattern of the tabernacle was revealed to Moses. After this pattern was given, the tabernacle was constructed and set up. Then by means of the priesthood and the offerings those who were condemned under the law were able to have fellowship with God. This fellowship was through the tabernacle, through Christ. This was a fulfillment in type, although not in reality, of God's promise to Abraham.

CHRIST FULFILLING THE PROMISE

We have considered three important persons: Adam, Abraham, and Moses. Now we come to a fourth person, the most important of all — Jesus Christ, who came to fulfill God's promise to Abraham. Christ fulfilled this promise according to the righteous requirements of the law given through Moses. In this way, He brought God's chosen people out from under the curse. Therefore, the promise became not only a covenant, but also a testament, a will, for everything that had been promised was accomplished. The requirements of the law were met, the curse was removed, and the promise was fulfilled. Now in this unique seed of Abraham all the divided and cursed nations are blessed. Today Christ, our good land, is the all-inclusive Spirit for our enjoyment. With Adam there was the curse, with Abraham there was the promise, with Moses there was the law, and with Christ there is the fulfillment of the promise. Now we, the believers, those of the household of faith, enjoy the new testament. Those of the household of faith are the church people. We are not those who work — we are those who hear. As members of the household of faith, we have the hearing of faith and thereby inherit, partake of, and experience the Triune God as our blessing. By the hearing of faith we have become people of faith, the household of faith. The more we hear, the more our faith is strengthened, and the more our capacity to enjoy the blessing is enlarged.

In the Bible there are six outstanding names or titles: Adam, Abraham, Moses, Christ, the church, and the New Jerusalem. God's intention in eternity past was not related to the law. His thought was focused not on the law, but on Adam, Abraham, Christ, the church, and the New Jerusalem, the ultimate consummation of God's work with man. Today we are in the church; in eternity we shall be in the New Jerusalem. God uses the law temporarily to expose His people, who do not have the proper knowledge of themselves and their condition. He also uses the law as a custodian to guard and keep the people and as an escort, a child conductor, to bring them to Christ. But once the law has fulfilled its function of bringing us to Christ, the law should not be allowed to stand in the way. Moses was not only the one through whom the law was given; he was also the one to receive the pattern of the tabernacle and under whose leadership it was set up.

It is significant that from Adam to Abraham is approximately two thousand years and that from Abraham to Christ is approximately another two thousand years. Furthermore, it has been almost two thousand years since the Lord appeared on earth as a man. I find it very difficult to believe that the church age will continue another thousand years. After the church age, there will be the kingdom age, which will last a thousand years. After that, we shall be in eternity. I dare not say that the seven days in Genesis 1 typify the seven thousand years which may cover the time from Adam to the end of the millennium. However, it is very meaningful that from the fall to the giving of the promise was about two thousand years, that from the giving of the promise to the coming of Christ for the fulfillment of the promise was another two thousand years, and that the age of fulfillment has lasted for approximately yet another two thousand years. Although we look forward to the kingdom age, we will not be satisfied just with the kingdom. The thousand year period of the millennium will be in the eyes of God as one day. Thus, our aspiration is to enter into the New Jerusalem for eternity.

In the fulfillment of God's eternal purpose, the law has only a temporary place. It was given four hundred thirty years after God's promise was made to Abraham. With the coming of Christ the law was fulfilled and terminated.

GRACE AND FAITH

Faith is not related to the law, but related to grace. Our faith is the reflection of the grace of Christ. Faith functions like a camera, which is used to photograph a particular scene. The grace of Christ is the scenery, and our faith is the camera which takes the picture. Thus, our faith becomes the reflection of the grace of Christ. In other words, our faith is the reflection of God's promise in its fulfillment.

Faith has nothing to do with the law. The Galatians were mistaken in giving place to the law once again and allowing it to be brought into the way. The law must no longer be in the scene. Instead, our camera of faith should be focused fully on grace. Instead of trying to keep the law, we should use our faith to photograph the scenery of grace. Now in faith we are enjoying grace, which is the Triune God processed to become the all-inclusive life-giving Spirit for our enjoyment. How wonderful! The curse has been taken away, and the law has been set aside. Now we have the unique fulfillment of God's promise, which has become the blessing to all believers. We are believing Abrahams enjoying God's promise in a full way. If we see this and understand it, we shall realize that the promise is versus the law. No longer is there any ground, position, or place for the law. The law has been taken out of the way. Praise the Lord that our camera of faith is photographing the scenery of grace!

LIFE-STUDY OF GALATIANS

FAITH REPLACING LAW

Scripture Reading: Gal. 3:6-7, 9-10, 19a, 23-25; 4:2-3;
Rom. 2:12; 7:5; John 3:18; 16:9; 3:36; Acts 16:31; Rom.
16:26; 2 Tim. 4:7b; Jude 3, 20; John 3:15; Acts 6:7;
1 Tim. 3:9

In the foregoing message we saw that the promise is versus the law. In this message we shall see that faith replaces law.

In 3:5 Paul asks, "He therefore Who is supplying to you the Spirit and doing works of power among you, is it by the works of law or by the hearing of faith?" The Spirit in this verse is the all-inclusive, compound Spirit, typified by the compound ointment in Exodus 30:23-25. It is the Spirit mentioned in John 7:39, who is the life-imparting Christ in resurrection. This Spirit is the bountiful supply to the believers in God's New Testament economy. We receive this Spirit not by the works of law, but by faith in the crucified and glorified Christ.

In verse 6 Paul goes on to say, "Even as Abraham believed God, and it was reckoned to him for righteousness." The bewitched Galatians, by drifting back to the law, were clinging to Moses, through whom the law was given. But Paul referred them to Abraham, who was the father of faith. Faith was of God's original economy; the law was later added because of transgressions (v. 19). After Christ fulfilled the law through His death, God wanted His people to return to His original economy. With Abraham it was not a matter of keeping the law, but a matter of believing God. It should be so with all the New Testament believers.

In verses 9 and 10 Paul says, "So that they who are of

faith are blessed with believing Abraham. For as many as are of the works of law are under a curse; for it is written, Cursed is everyone who does not abide by all the things written in the book of the law to do them." Faith in Christ brings us into the blessing God promised to Abraham, which is the promise of the Spirit (v. 14). This faith had brought the Galatian believers into the blessing in Christ. They were enjoying the grace of life in the Spirit. But the Judaizers bewitched them and caused them to come under the curse of the law, thus depriving them of the enjoyment of Christ and causing them to fall from grace (5:4).

According to verse 8, the promise God gave to Abraham, "In you all nations shall be blessed," was the gospel. It was preached to him not only before the accomplishing of redemption by Christ, but also before the giving of the law through Moses. What God promised to Abraham corresponds to what God accomplished in Christ, which is the fulfillment of His promise to Abraham. The New Testament economy is a continuation of His dealing with Abraham and has nothing to do with the law of Moses. All the New Testament believers should be in this continuation and should have nothing to do with the law given through Moses.

I. LAW

A. God's Principle in Dealing with Man
in the Old Testament Economy

Law was the principle according to which God dealt with His people in the Old Testament economy. In dealing with the children of Israel according to the law, God dealt with them through the tabernacle with the priesthood and the offerings. On the one hand, He dealt with them according to the law; on the other hand, He dealt with them through the tabernacle. After the giving of the law, God came to dwell in the tabernacle. At the end of the book of Exodus, the tabernacle was set up. Then at the very beginning of Leviticus, we see that God spoke from within the tent of meeting. God was hidden within the tabernacle and spoke in the tabernacle. Thus, God dealt with His people from within the tabernacle, through the tabernacle, and according to the law.

Suppose an Israelite committed a certain sin. According to the law, that one had to be condemned, perhaps even put to death. The law exposed his sin and condemned him. However, the sinner could present a trespass offering, which was then offered on the altar by the priest. In this way the one who had sinned could be forgiven. After the law exposed and condemned him, it brought him to the tabernacle through the altar. This indicates that the law first exposes us and then brings us unto Christ. If there had been no law to condemn the people, there would have been no need of redemption. We need redemption because we are under the condemnation of the law. By exposing and condemning us, the law brings us to Christ.

The law is a custodian which keeps sinners by condemning them. Apart from the law's condemnation, it could not function as a custodian. Without the law's exposure and condemnation, we cannot realize how many sins we have committed against God. Without the law, we would be without regulation or restriction. But because the law condemns us, we are kept by the law.

In keeping us by condemning us, the law brings us to Christ. In the Old Testament, an Israelite who had sinned was condemned by the law and required to bring a trespass offering. The law functioned as a custodian to bring the sinning Israelite to Christ, his Redeemer, typified by the trespass offering. In this way the law keeps us and brings us to Christ.

On the one hand, Paul put the law in the position of Hagar, Abraham's concubine. On the other hand, the law has a positive position, that of a custodian to keep us and that of a child-conductor to bring us to Christ. We should not return to the law. To do this is to go to Hagar. However, we should not despise the law either, for it serves as a warden to care for those who are weak or childish. In its role as a child-conductor, the law takes care of the child. It does this by convicting, judging, condemning, and exposing the child. When the child is tempted to do something wrong, the law rebukes him and condemns him in order to keep him and to bring him to the proper place. Therefore, by exposing us and condemning us, the law serves as a child-conductor to bring us to Christ.

We have pointed out that the law was the basic principle according to which God dealt with His people in the Old Testament. If it were not for the law, not many of the children of Israel would have come to the altar with a trespass offering. Because the law exposed them and condemned them, they realized their need to come to the altar with the required offering. In this, the law is very useful to God. Although God dealt with His people according to the law, He did not deal with them through the law, but dealt with them through the tabernacle.

B. To Expose Man's Fallen Condition

In 3:19 Paul tells us that the law "was added because of transgressions." The law was not an original part of God's economy. It was added while God's economy was proceeding because of man's transgression, until the seed, Christ, should come, to whom God's promise was made. Since it was added because of man's transgressions, it should have been deducted when those transgressions were taken away. Because Christ, the seed, has come, the law must be terminated. Its function is to expose man's fallen condition.

C. To Keep Man in Its Custody for Christ

In 3:23 Paul says, "But before faith came we were guarded under law, being shut up unto the faith which was about to be revealed." To be guarded is to be kept in custody, kept in ward. To be guarded under law, by being shut up there, can be compared to sheep being enclosed in a fold (John 10:1, 16). In God's economy, the law was used as a fold to keep God's chosen people until Christ came. Because Christ has come, God's people should no longer be kept under the law.

The Greek word rendered "unto" in 3:23 can also be translated "with a view to." This indicates that the shutting up has an objective or goal in view. It should result in bringing the guarded people to the faith.

In caring for their children, Christian parents need to preach the law to them. We should not first preach grace to the children. If we give them regulations according to the law, the law will keep them in custody for Christ. Thus, we should first give them the law in a strong way. The law will expose them, guard them, and keep them, serving as a custodian to keep them for Christ.

D. To Conduct Man unto Christ

In 3:24 Paul continues, "So the law has become our child-conductor unto Christ, that we might be justified by faith." The Greek word for "child-conductor" can also be rendered escort, guardian, or custodian. It denotes one who cares for a child who is under age and conducts him to the schoolmaster. The law was used by God as a custodian, a guardian, a child-conductor, to watch over His chosen people before Christ came, and to escort and conduct them to Christ at the proper time.

Galatians 3:25 says, "But faith having come, we are no longer under a child-conductor." Since faith in Christ has come, we do not need to be under the guarding law any longer.

As a child-conductor, the law brings us unto Christ that we may be justified by faith. When an Israelite came to the altar with a trespass offering, he was justified by faith in that offering. Because of the trespass offering, God forgave him of his sin. The Israelite was justified not by works of law, but by his faith in the trespass offering. In typology, this is to be justified by faith. The principle in the New Testament is the same. The law still condemns all those who have sinned. Those condemned under the law should come to Christ and exercise faith in Him as their trespass offering. In this way, sinners are justified by faith.

E. Related to the Flesh

The law is related to the flesh. This is indicated in Romans 7:5, where Paul says, "For when we were in the flesh, the passions of sins, which were through the law, operated in our members to bear fruit to death." The works of the law are always related to the flesh. A believer's efforts to keep the law are not of the Spirit, but are of the flesh. Even if someone has the intention to please God by fulfilling the requirements of the law, that intention will cause him to be involved with the flesh.

In Romans 7 Paul tells us that the law is good, even spiritual. Thus, we have no right to find fault with the law. Instead, we should blame our flesh. Whenever we try to keep the law, we exercise the flesh.

F. The Works of Law Being under the Curse

In Galatians 3:10 Paul says, "For as many as are of the works of law are under a curse; for it is written, Cursed is everyone who does not abide by all the things written in the book of the law to do them." If we try to keep the law, we shall be in the flesh and automatically be under the curse, for the works of the law are under the curse. Instead of trying to keep the law, we should thank the law for exposing us and condemning us and then bid it farewell. We should not form a permanent relationship with the law. We should leave the law and go to Christ and to the cross. If we stay in the flesh with the law, we shall remain under the curse. But if we go to Christ and the cross, we shall be justified by faith.

II. FAITH

It is difficult to understand faith in a full way. In Acts 6:7 we are told that many priests were obedient to the faith, and in 2 Timothy 4:7 Paul says that he kept the faith. According to Jude 3, we must contend for the faith once delivered to the saints. Furthermore, Paul charged the deacons to hold the mystery of the faith (1 Tim. 3:9). We can define faith in different ways. We may say that faith is a camera which photographs the scenery of grace. Faith is also the reflection of grace, and it is the appreciation of grace with the calling, receiving, accepting, joining, partaking, and enjoying.

A. God's Principle in Dealing with Man in His New Testament Economy

Just as the law was the basic principle according to which God dealt with His people in the Old Testament, faith is the basic principle according to which He deals with people in the New Testament. All those who refuse to believe in Christ will perish, whereas those who believe in Him will be forgiven of their sins and receive eternal life. In John 16:9 we are told that the Spirit will convict the world concerning sin because of not believing in the Son of God. This indicates that the unique sin which causes people to perish is unbelief. God's commandment to sinners is to believe in the Son of God.

In the New Testament the term faith is all-inclusive. It has both a divine aspect and a human aspect, for it implies something on God's side and something on our side. On God's side, the term "the faith" implies that God sent His Son to earth, that Christ died on the cross to accomplish redemption, that He was buried and was resurrected, that in resurrection He released the divine life and has become the life-giving Spirit — all that He might enter into all those who believe in Him to be grace, life, power, sanctification, and everything to them. On our side, faith is related to hearing, appreciating, calling, receiving, accepting, joining, partaking, and enjoying. Furthermore, faith involves rejoicing, thanking, praising, and overflowing. Faith hears and appreciates. Faith calls, receives, and accepts. Faith also joins, partakes, enjoys, rejoices, gives thanks, and praises. Therefore, faith results in the overflow of life from within us.

If we do not have faith, all that has been accomplished on God's side will remain objective and not be personally related to us. We need our faith to function as a camera to photograph the scenery of grace. For faith to operate in this way implies that we apprehend the divine scenery by hearing, appreciating, calling, receiving, accepting, joining, partaking, enjoying, rejoicing, thanking, praising, and overflowing.

Faith is actually the all-inclusive Triune God infused into our being. This infusion takes place as we are under the preaching of grace and hear the word of grace. When the processed Triune God is infused into us, He becomes our faith. This faith is the reflection of grace. Therefore, grace and faith, faith and grace, are two ends of one thing.

Neither grace nor faith has anything to do with the law. Today God deals with people not according to law, but according to faith. We need to keep this faith, turn to it, obey it, and contend for it.

B. The Principle by Which God Dealt with Abraham

In 3:6, 7, and 9 we see that faith was the principle by which God dealt with Abraham. Verse 9 says, "So that they who are of faith are blessed with believing Abraham." Under God's dealing, Abraham was not working to please God; instead, he was believing Him.

C. Our Believing in Christ, Taking His Person and Redemptive Work As the Object of Our Faith

On the one hand, faith is our believing in Christ. On the other hand, it is our taking Christ's Person and redemptive work as the object of our faith (John 3:36; Acts 16:31; Rom. 16:26; 2 Tim. 4:7b; Jude 3, 20).

D. Replacing Law

Faith replaces law (Gal. 3:23, 25). Since faith has come, we should not stay with the law any longer. The law kept us and brought us to Christ, but now in our experience it should be replaced by faith.

E. Bringing Us into the Blessing Promised to Abraham

We have pointed out that 3:9 says that "they who are of faith are blessed with believing Abraham." Faith brings us into the blessing God promised to Abraham, that is, to the all-inclusive land which typifies the all-inclusive Spirit. Hence, faith in Christ brings us the promise of the Spirit (3:14).

F. Ushering Us into Christ

Furthermore, faith ushers us into Christ. According to John 3:15, everyone who believes in Christ, or into Christ (Gk.), has eternal life.

G. Characterizing the Believers in Christ and Distinguishing Them from the Keepers of Law

Finally, faith characterizes those who believe in Christ, and it distinguishes them from those who keep the law (Acts 6:7; 1 Tim. 3:9). We are not keepers of law — we are believers in Christ. We are the people of faith.

In 3:7 and 9 Paul speaks of those "who are of faith." According to both Darby's *New Translation* and the Chinese version, this expression denotes the principle of faith. These versions adopt the rendering "on the principle of faith." To be of faith means to be on the principle of faith. We are those who take faith as our principle. Everything we do should be in keeping with this principle. By this principle we come to Christ, receive Him, and become one with Him.

Galatians 3:23 and 25 say that faith has come. This is another strong expression. Once we were guarded under law, but now faith has come. This means that the processed Triune God as grace has come. The coming of faith also includes the coming of appreciation, receiving, and rejoicing. This is the faith which replaces law!

LIFE-STUDY OF GALATIANS

THE SEED OF ABRAHAM
AND THE SONS OF ABRAHAM

Scripture Reading: Gal. 3:7, 9, 16, 19, 26-29

In Galatians 3 Paul speaks of the seed of Abraham (vv. 16, 19, 29) and the sons of Abraham (v. 7). The seed is singular, whereas the sons are plural. It is rather difficult for many readers of Galatians to understand the significance of this.

Concerning God's promise to Abraham, there is the aspect of fulfillment and the aspect of enjoyment. To fulfill the promise is one thing, but to enjoy the blessing of the promise is another. Concerning promises made by one person to another, the one who fulfills the promise is seldom the one who enjoys the blessing of the promise. Usually the person who makes the promise is the one to fulfill the promise, and the one to whom the promise is made is the one who enjoys its blessing. In the case of God's promise to Abraham, God, strictly speaking, is not the one to fulfill the promise. Instead, the promise is fulfilled by the seed, Christ (v. 16). Christ has fulfilled God's promise to Abraham. Thus, the fulfillment of this promise does not depend on the many sons of Abraham, but on the unique seed of Abraham. However, with respect to the enjoyment of the blessing of this promise, the many sons are involved. Whereas the unique seed is the fulfiller, the many sons are the enjoyers. If we understand this matter, we shall be able to understand what Paul is talking about in Galatians 3.

Paul wrote the third chapter of Galatians as if he were an attorney writing a legal document. His wording is specific and precise. Consider verse 16: "But to Abraham were the promises spoken and to his seed. He does not say, And to the seeds, as concerning many, but as concerning one,

And to your seed, Who is Christ." In verses 19 and 29 Paul also refers to the seed. But in verse 26 he speaks of the sons of God. The sons of Abraham in verse 7 are the sons of God in verse 26. Now we must ask how the many sons of Abraham can be the many sons of God. The answer to this question involves the seed. On the one hand, the seed is the heir who inherits the promise. However, as the seed of Abraham, Christ also fulfills the promise.

The children of Israel, the descendants of Abraham, inherited the good land of Canaan. In typology, the good land signifies Christ. Christ is both the seed and the land. He is not only the seed inheriting the promise; He is also the good land. Both the seed and the good land are types of Christ. As the unique seed in Galatians 3, Christ not only inherits the promise, but He also fulfills the promise. The promise God made to Abraham was fulfilled by Christ as Abraham's seed.

In the matter of fulfilling the promise, we have no part. Only Christ, the unique seed, is qualified to fulfill God's promise to Abraham. In this sense, the seed is uniquely one. But in the aspect of enjoying the fulfilled promise, the seed becomes many, the many sons of Abraham.

I. THE SEED OF ABRAHAM

A. Only One — Christ

We know from 3:16 that Christ is Abraham's unique seed. Christ is the seed, and the seed is the heir who inherits the promises. Here, Christ is the unique seed inheriting the promises. Hence, in order to inherit the promised blessing, we must be one with Christ. Outside of Him, we cannot inherit the promises given by God to Abraham. In God's eyes Abraham has only one seed, Christ. We must be in Him that we may participate in the promise given to Abraham. He is not only the seed inheriting the promise, but also the blessing of the promise for inheritance. For the Galatian believers to turn back from Christ to the law meant that they would forfeit both the Heir and the inheritance of the promises.

If Christ had not come, there would have been no way for God to fulfill His promise to Abraham. As we have pointed out, the One who fulfilled this promise is not the One who made the promise, but the promised One, the seed. God had promised to give Abraham both a seed and the good land. This promise was fulfilled by the unique, promised seed.

B. Including All the Believers
Who Have Been Baptized into Him

As the unique seed of Abraham, Christ includes all the believers who have been baptized into Him (3:27-28). In one sense, when Christ died on the cross, He was crucified alone as our Redeemer. But in another sense, when He was crucified, we were with Him. For the accomplishment of redemption, Christ was crucified alone. But for terminating the old creation, Christ included us in His crucifixion. In the same principle, in the fulfillment of the promise made by God to Abraham, we are not included as part of the unique seed. We can have no share in the fulfillment of this promise. However, for inheriting the promise and enjoying it, we are included. Christ alone fulfilled the promise. But Christ and we share in the enjoyment of the promise. Therefore, on the one hand, the seed is uniquely one; on the other hand, it is all-inclusive. For fulfillment, the seed is one; for inheritance and enjoyment, the seed is all-inclusive, including all believers who have been baptized into Christ.

C. To Whom the Promise Was Made
before the Law Was Given

In 3:19 we see that the promise was made to the seed before the law was given. The promise was made not to the many sons, but to the seed who fulfilled the promise.

D. The Unique Seed Being the Good Land

The unique seed is also the good land. The seed here is not only for the fulfillment of the promise, but also for the inheritance of the promise. To inherit the promise is to inherit the good land. The unique seed is the land. This proves that the seed is also the one to fulfill the promise, not only the one to inherit the promise. If He were only the one to inherit the promise, who then is the land?

II. THE SONS OF ABRAHAM

A. Of Faith, Based upon the Principle of Faith

Galatians 3:7 says, "Know then that they who are of faith, these are sons of Abraham." Works of law make people disciples of Moses (John 9:28) with nothing whatever related to life. Faith in Christ makes the New Testament believers sons of God, a relationship altogether in life. We, the New Testament believers, were born sons of fallen Adam, and in Adam, because of transgressions, we were under the law of Moses. But we have been reborn to become sons of Abraham and have been freed from the law of Moses by faith in Christ. We are sons of Abraham not by natural birth, but by faith. Hence, our being sons of Abraham is based upon the principle of faith. It is based on our believing, not on our working. Our basis for being sons of Abraham surely is not natural descent. We are Abraham's sons according to the principle of faith.

B. Blessed with Believing Abraham

In verse 9 Paul goes on to say, "So that they who are of faith are blessed with believing Abraham." Under God's dealing, Abraham was not working to please God. He was believing Him. Now we who are of faith are blessed with believing Abraham.

C. Sons of God through Faith in Christ

Faith is the reflection of grace. We may also say that faith is a photograph of the divine scenery. Through such faith we become true sons of Abraham. When we believed in Christ, an organic union took place. The divine life entered into us, and we were born of God through faith. As our faith photographed the divine scenery of grace, something of a real and substantial spiritual nature was infused into us. Although this substance is neither material nor physical, it is nonetheless very real. Faith is not superstition. It is related to substantial spiritual reality, a reality which admittedly is very mysterious. This reality is actually the processed Triune God Himself. When we exercise faith in Christ and thereby take a spiritual photograph of the divine scenery, the processed God enters into our being to be our life. This life is divine, spiritual, heavenly, and holy. Entering into us, it causes a spiritual birth to take place. This birth brings about an organic union between us and the Triune God. Because God has been born into our being, we have become sons of God. Thus, we may say that we are God-men.

Some Christians oppose the use of the term God-men and even defame us for saying that the believers in Christ, the sons of God through faith in Christ, are God-men. But according to the Bible, it is a divine fact that human beings can become sons of God. When we believed in Christ, the divine life with the divine nature — in fact, the divine Being of the Triune God Himself — entered into us, and we were born of God to become sons of God. Just as a man's son partakes of his life and nature, so we as God's sons partake of the divine life and nature. The offspring of a tiger is a tiger. In the same principle, God's offspring are His sons possessing the divine life and the divine nature.

Certain early church fathers went so far as to speak of the "deification" of the believers in Christ. I would advise against the use of such a term. To say that the believers are deified to become objects of worship is blasphemy. But it is correct to say that the believers are deified in the sense of possessing the divine life and the divine nature. If at all possible, we should replace the word deification with a more suitable term to convey the fact that we have been born of God to become sons of God. Praise the Lord that God is our Father and that we are the same as He with respect to the divine life and nature! However, we emphatically state that we shall never be the same as God in the sense of deserving to be worshipped. It is blasphemy to claim that, as sons of God, we should be worshipped along

with God. But it is not too much to say that because we are
sons of God, we have the very life and nature of our Father.
Far from being blasphemy, it is a glory to the Father to declare this fact.

Now we must go on to ask in what way the sons of God
are also the sons of Abraham. Christ is both the Son of God
and the Son of Abraham. Because we are now in Christ, we
are sons of God on the one hand and sons of Abraham on
the other hand. How can we be sons of God? Because we
are in Christ, who is the Son of God. How can we be sons of
Abraham? Also because we are in Christ, who is the Son of
Abraham.

It is a matter of tremendous significance for the divine
life to be imparted into us. This impartation of the divine
life causes an organic union which makes us both the sons
of God and the sons of Abraham. This organic union takes
place exclusively in Christ. In Christ we enjoy the wonderful organic union with the Triune God. In this union we
are, on the one hand, the sons of God and, on the other
hand, the sons of Abraham. Christ is the unique sphere in
which this all takes place. When we enter into this sphere,
we become sons of God and sons of Abraham. Our true
status is that in Christ and by the organic union we are
both sons of God and sons of Abraham.

D. Baptized into Christ and Putting On Christ

We are both sons of Abraham and sons of God because
we have been baptized into Christ and have put on Christ
(3:27). To believe is to believe into Christ (John 3:16), and
to be baptized is to be baptized also into Christ. Faith in
Christ brings us into Christ and makes us one with Christ,
in whom is the sonship. We must be identified with Christ
through faith so that in Him we may be sons of God. By
both faith and baptism, we have been immersed into
Christ, we have thus put on Christ, and we have become
identified with Him.

Although we all have a natural life with a natural
ancestry, we need not live any longer according to that life.
Instead, we may live by the divine life with the divine

nature. By living according to this life, we are in reality the sons of God and the sons of Abraham. We have been baptized into Christ, the unique seed who has fulfilled God's promise to Abraham. We and Christ have been joined in a marvelous organic union. Because of this union, we are sons of God and sons of Abraham. Here in this organic union we inherit the promise which has been fulfilled by Christ. Actually, Christ Himself is this inheritance. The promise we inherit is the promise we now enjoy.

E. All One in Christ

Galatians 3:28 says, "There cannot be Jew nor Greek, there cannot be slave nor free man, there cannot be male and female; for you are all one in Christ Jesus." Here we see that the sons of Abraham are all one in Christ, without any natural status. In Christ there are no differences among races and nationalities, in social rank, or between the sexes.

F. Included in Abraham's Only Seed

Galatians 3:29 says, "And if you are Christ's, then you are Abraham's seed, heirs according to promise." Abraham's seed is only one, Christ (v. 16). Hence, to be Abraham's seed we must be Christ's, a part of Christ. Because we are one with Christ, we are also Abraham's seed, heirs according to promise, inheriting God's promised blessing, which is the all-inclusive Spirit as the ultimate consummation of the processed God to be our portion. Under the New Testament, the believers as God's chosen people, being sons of full age, are such heirs, not under law but in Christ. The Judaizers who remained under law and kept themselves apart from Christ were, like Ishmael (4:23), Abraham's descendants according to flesh, not, like Isaac (4:28), his heirs according to promise. But the believers in Christ are such heirs, inheriting the promised blessing. Hence, we should remain in Christ and not turn to law.

Since the law is unable to give us life (3:21), it cannot produce the sons of God. But the Spirit that is received by faith (3:2) and that gives us life (2 Cor. 3:6) can produce the sons of God. Law kept God's chosen people under its custody until faith came (3:23). Faith in Christ as the all-inclusive life-giving Spirit makes God's chosen people Abraham's seed as "the stars of the heavens" (Gen. 22:17) according to God's promise.

Now we are in a position to see a brief sketch of Galatians 3. This chapter reveals that God intended to give the promise to Abraham according to His eternal purpose. Before this promise was accomplished, the law was given to serve as the custodian of God's chosen people. Then, at the appointed time, Christ, the promised seed, came to fulfill God's promise to Abraham. When Christ came, the fulfillment of God's promised blessing also came. This is grace. Hence, grace came with Christ and with the fulfillment. All this is on God's side. On our side, we need a way to apprehend, realize, and grasp all that Christ, the seed, has accomplished. In other words, we need a spiritual camera to photograph the scenery of grace. This "camera" is our faith. Therefore, with the coming of grace on God's side, there is also the coming of faith on our side. Now that we have grace, faith, and the seed which has fulfilled the promise, we no longer need the law to serve as our custodian. Hence, the law should be set aside. It should no longer have any place in the scenery. We must turn from the law, the custodian, and stay with Christ, the One who has fulfilled the promise. Of course, this means we should also stay with grace and faith. Then we shall be included in Christ, the unique seed, to inherit the fulfilled promise and to enjoy the blessing of the promise to Abraham. This blessing is the processed Triune God as the all-inclusive life-giving Spirit.

LIFE-STUDY OF GALATIANS

BAPTIZED INTO CHRIST, PUTTING ON CHRIST, AND ALL ONE IN CHRIST

Scripture Reading: Gal. 3:27-29; Rom. 6:3; Matt. 28:19b; 1 Cor. 12:13a; Rom. 13:14; Eph. 2:15-16; Col. 3:10-11

In this message we shall consider 3:27-29. In 3:26 Paul tells us that we "are all sons of God through faith in Christ Jesus." Verse 27 opens with the word for, which connects these verses and indicates that verse 27 gives an explanation of how we are sons of God through faith in Christ Jesus. We are sons of God because we are in Christ, and we are in Christ because we have been baptized into Christ. Verse 27 says, "For as many as were baptized into Christ have put on Christ." To be baptized into Christ is the way to be in Christ. Based upon the fact that we have been baptized into Christ, we can say that we have put on Christ.

In verse 28 Paul continues, "There cannot be Jew nor Greek, there cannot be slave nor free man, there cannot be male and female; for you are all one in Christ Jesus." Here we see that we are one in Christ with His resurrection life and His divine nature to be the one new man, as mentioned in Ephesians 2:15. This new man is absolutely in Christ. There is no room for our natural being, our natural disposition, or our natural character. In this one new man Christ is all and in all (Col. 3:10-11).

In Romans 6:3 Paul says, "Or are you ignorant that as many as have been baptized into Christ Jesus have been baptized into His death?" Here we see that when we were baptized into Christ Jesus, we were also baptized into the death of Christ. On the one hand, we have been baptized into Christ's person; on the other hand, we have been baptized into Christ's death.

In Matthew 28:19 the Lord Jesus gave a charge to His disciples: "Go therefore and disciple all the nations, baptizing them into the name of the Father and of the Son and of the Holy Spirit." According to this verse, the believers are baptized into the name of the Triune God, into the name of the Father, Son, and Holy Spirit. Later we shall consider what it means to baptize, to immerse, someone into the name of the Triune God.

In 1 Corinthians 12:13 we see yet another aspect of baptism: "For in one Spirit were we all baptized into one body, whether we be Jews or Gentiles, whether we be bond or free, and were all made to drink of one Spirit" (Gk.). According to this verse, we have also been baptized into the Body.

In Ephesians 2:15 and 16 Paul says, "Having abolished in His flesh the law of the commandments in ordinances, that He might create the two in Himself into one new man, making peace, and might reconcile both in one Body to God through the cross, slaying the enmity by it." In these verses we have the thought that all believers, Jews and Gentiles alike, have been reconciled to God in one Body and in Christ have been created into one new man. In Colossians 3:10 and 11 Paul says, "And having put on the new man, who is being renewed unto full knowledge according to the image of Him Who created him; where there cannot be Greek and Jew, circumcision and uncircumcision, barbarian, Scythian, slave, freeman, but Christ is all and in all."

I. BAPTIZED INTO CHRIST

We have seen that at the end of Galatians 3 Paul tells us that we have all been baptized into Christ. This is the main factor in our being the sons of God and the sons of Abraham. It is also the factor by which we are included in the seed of Abraham, and in addition the factor which brings us into the enjoyment of the blessing of God's promise through faith. Because we have been baptized into Christ, we now enjoy an organic union with Him.

Concerning baptism, the New Testament reveals that

we have been baptized into the name of the Father, Son, and Holy Spirit (Matt. 28:19), into Christ (Gal. 3:27), into the death of Christ (Rom. 6:3), and into the Body of Christ (1 Cor. 12:13). We need to exercise our entire being in order to have a proper understanding of such a wonderful baptism. Regrettably, many Christians today do not have an adequate view of baptism. Some Christians argue about the method of baptism or about the kind of water used. Some reduce baptism to a dead ritual. Other Christians go to another extreme and associate baptism with speaking in tongues. Rarely among today's Christians do we see baptism practiced in a proper, genuine, and living way, with the believers baptized into the name of the Triune God, into Christ, into the death of Christ, and into the Body of Christ. Such a baptism, a baptism into the divine name, a living Person, an effective death, and a living organism, puts the believers into a position where they can experience an organic union with Christ.

Commenting on Matthew 28:19 in his *Word Studies in the New Testament*, M. R. Vincent says, "Baptizing into the name of the Holy Trinity implies a spiritual and mystical union with him." The Greek preposition rendered "into" is crucial, for it points to this spiritual, mystical union. Moreover, Vincent says that the word "name" here "is the expression of the sum total of the divine Being. . . . It is equivalent to his *person*." Therefore, to baptize believers into the name of the Triune God means to baptize them into the very being, the Person, of the Triune God. The name denotes the Person, and the Person is the all-inclusive, processed Triune God as the life-giving Spirit. When we baptize people into the name of the Triune God, we baptize them into such a divine Person. To baptize anyone into the name of the Trinity is to immerse that one into all the Triune God is.

According to the Gospel of Matthew, baptism brings repentant people out of their old state into a new one, by terminating their old life and germinating them with the new life of Christ that they may become the kingdom people. John the Baptist's recommending ministry began with a preliminary baptism by water only. Now, after the heavenly King accomplished His ministry on earth, passed through the process of death and resurrection, and became the life-giving Spirit, He charged His disciples to baptize the ones they discipled into the Triune God. This baptism has two aspects: the visible aspect by water, and the invisible aspect by the Holy Spirit (Acts 2:38, 41; 10:44-48). The visible aspect is the expression, the testimony, of the invisible aspect; whereas the invisible aspect is the reality of the visible aspect. Without the invisible aspect by the Spirit, the visible aspect by water is vain; and without the visible aspect by water, the invisible aspect by the Spirit is abstract and impractical. Both are needed. Not long after the Lord charged the disciples with this baptism, He baptized them and the entire church in the Holy Spirit (1 Cor. 12:13) on the day of Pentecost (Acts 1:5; 2:4) and in the house of Cornelius (Acts 11:15-17). Then, based upon this, the disciples baptized the new converts (Acts 2:38), not only visibly into water, but also invisibly into the death of Christ (Rom. 6:3-4), into Christ Himself (Gal. 3:27), into the Triune God (Matt. 28:19), and into the Body of Christ (1 Cor. 12:13). The water, signifying the death of Christ with His burial, may be considered a tomb to terminate the old history of the one being baptized. Since the death of Christ is included in Christ, and since Christ is the very embodiment of the Triune God, and the Triune God is eventually one with the Body of Christ, so to baptize new believers into the death of Christ, into Christ Himself, into the Triune God, and into the Body of Christ is to terminate their old life, on the negative side, and, on the positive side, to germinate them with new life, the eternal life of the Triune God, for the Body of Christ. Hence, the baptism ordained by the Lord in Matthew 28:19 is one that baptizes people out of their life into the Body life for the kingdom of the heavens.

We have pointed out that the Greek word rendered "into" indicates union, as in Romans 6:3; Galatians 3:27; and 1 Corinthians 12:13. The same Greek word is used in Acts 8:16; 19:3, 5; and 1 Corinthians 1:13, 15. To baptize people into the name of the Triune God is to bring them into spiritual and mystical union with Him.

Matthew and John are the two books in which the Trinity is more fully revealed, for the participation and enjoyment of God's chosen people, than in all other books of Scripture. John unveils the mystery of the Godhead in the Father, Son, and Spirit, especially in chapters fourteen through sixteen, for our experience of life; whereas Matthew makes known the reality of the Trinity in the one name for all Three, for the constitution of the kingdom. In the opening chapter of Matthew, the Holy Spirit (v. 18), Christ (the Son — v. 18), and God (the Father — v. 23) are all on the scene for the producing of the man Jesus (v. 21), who, as Jehovah the Savior and God with us, is the very embodiment of the Triune God. In chapter three Matthew presents a picture of the Son standing in the water of baptism under the opened heaven, the Spirit as a dove descending upon the Son, and the Father out of the heavens speaking to the Son (vv. 16-17). In chapter twelve, the Son, in the person of man, cast out demons by the Spirit to bring in the kingdom of God the Father (v. 28). In chapter sixteen, the Son is revealed by the Father to the disciples for the building of the church, which is the life-pulse of the kingdom (vv. 16-19). In chapter seventeen, the Son entered into transfiguration (v. 2) and was confirmed by the Father's word of delight (v. 5) for a miniature display of the manifestation of the kingdom (16:28). Eventually, in the closing chapter, after Christ, as the last Adam, had passed through the process of crucifixion, entered into the realm of resurrection, and become the life-giving Spirit, He came back to His disciples, in the atmosphere and reality of His resurrection, to charge them to cause the heathen to become the kingdom people by baptizing them into the name, the Person, the reality, of the Trinity. Later, in the Acts and in the Epistles, it is indicated that to baptize people into the name of the Father, Son, and Spirit is to baptize them into the name of Christ (Acts 8:16; 19:5, Gk.), and to baptize them into the name of Christ is to baptize them into Christ the Person (Gal.

3:27; Rom. 6:3), for Christ is the embodiment of the Triune
God, and He, as the life-giving Spirit, is available any time
and any place for people to be baptized into Him. Such a
baptism into the reality of the Father, Son, and Spirit,
according to Matthew, is for the constitution of the kingdom of the heavens. The heavenly kingdom cannot be
organized with human beings of flesh and blood (1 Cor.
15:50) as an earthly society. It can only be constituted with
people who are immersed into the union with the Triune
God and who are established and built up with the Triune
God who is wrought into them.

Whenever we are about to baptize people, we should
give them a rich, living message on the meaning of baptism. By hearing such a message, their faith will be stirred
up, and they will have a proper appreciation of baptism.
We should never baptize believers in a ritualistic way,
regarding baptism as a mere act of putting people into the
water according to the Bible. Such a baptism is void of the
reality of the organic union. But if people hear a rich word
on the meaning of baptism and have the hearing of faith,
they will earnestly desire to be baptized. Then, as we baptize them, we should exercise our faith to realize that we
are not only baptizing them into the water, but baptizing
them into a spiritual reality. As we immerse them into the
water, we immerse them into the Triune God as the all-
inclusive Spirit. When a person is baptized into the Triune
God, he enters into an organic union, which is able to
transform his whole being. By means of our organic union
with the Triune God, we are one with the Triune God, and
the Triune God is one with us.

II. PUTTING ON CHRIST

In Galatians 3:27 Paul says that as many as are baptized into Christ have put on Christ. To put on Christ is to
clothe ourselves with Christ, to put on Christ as a garment.
On the one hand, in baptism we are immersed into Christ;
on the other hand, in baptism we put on Christ. Christ, the
living Spirit, is the water of life. Hence, to be baptized into

Christ is to be immersed into Him as the Spirit. When a person is immersed into Christ, he automatically puts on Christ as his clothing. This means that the baptized one has become one with Christ, having been immersed into Him and having become clothed with Him.

If Christ were not the life-giving Spirit, there would be no way for us to be baptized into Christ. How could we be baptized into Christ if, according to the traditional teaching of the Trinity, He were only sitting in the heavens? For us to be baptized into Christ, Christ must be the *pneuma*, the air, the Spirit all around us. If we consider Christ simply as One in the heavens far away, we can practice baptism as a ritual. People can be baptized without any realization of the significance of baptism. However, we cannot be baptized into a Christ who is only in the heavens. But we can be baptized into the Christ who is the *pneuma*, the Spirit. This is proved by 1 Corinthians 12:13, where we are told that in one Spirit we were baptized into one Body. The Spirit here is the all-inclusive, processed Triune God. In the Spirit, the processed Triune God, we have been baptized into one Body. Therefore, for us to be baptized into such a divine reality, Christ must be the life-giving Spirit. Whenever we baptize others, we should tell them that the Triune God as the processed life-giving Spirit is all around them, and that they need to be baptized, immersed, into the reality of this divine Person.

It is significant that at the end of chapter three of Galatians Paul concludes with a word about being baptized into Christ and putting on Christ. The fact that Paul concludes with a word about baptism indicates that what he has covered in this chapter can be experienced only if we have been baptized into Christ and have put on Christ. We should not be concerned with whether or not we have spoken in tongues, but with whether or not we have been baptized into Christ and have put on Christ. Our concern should be that we have become one with Christ. I can testify strongly that I have been baptized into Christ and that I am wearing Him as my clothing, my covering. I have the full assurance that I am one with Him and that He is one with me. I have the divine life, I am in the divine Person, and the divine Person is one with me.

III. ALL ONE IN CHRIST

In verse 28 Paul says that in Christ there "cannot be Jew nor Greek, there cannot be slave nor free man, there cannot be male and female; for you are all one in Christ Jesus." This indicates that in Christ there is no place for the natural man. Because we have been baptized, the natural man has been terminated, buried, and is now in the tomb. All the differences among races and nationalities, in social rank, and between the sexes have been abolished, and we are all one in Christ Jesus.

The word "one" in 3:28 is of great significance. However, for the most part, today's Christians in their experience are not one. The reason for this lack of oneness is that so many have not experienced the proper and genuine baptism in which they are immersed into the Person of the Triune God, into Christ as the life-giving Spirit, into the death of Christ, and into the Body of Christ. Through baptism, we, the baptized ones, are one in Christ. If we take in such a word about baptism with the hearing of faith, we shall have the assurance to say that we are in the Triune God, in Christ, and in the Body of Christ. Furthermore, we shall know that we are one with all those who have been baptized into Christ.

By faith we reflect the divine scenery of grace. Our living has become a photograph in which others can see the heavenly things. Through us and in us, they can behold the heavenly reality. What we are reflecting today is not the law; it is Christ as the all-inclusive Spirit, the blessing of God's promise to Abraham. We are a reflection of the fact that we, the believers in Christ, are all one in Him.

LIFE-STUDY OF GALATIANS

MESSAGE TWENTY-TWO

THE SPIRIT OF SONSHIP
REPLACING THE CUSTODY OF THE LAW

Scripture Reading: Gal. 3:27-29; 4:1-7; Rom. 8:14-16

In the foregoing message we pointed out that Paul concludes Galatians 3 with three important matters: baptized into Christ, putting on Christ, and the oneness of all the believers in Christ. To be baptized into Christ is to enter into an organic union with the Triune God. God's intention in His economy is to put us into Him and to come into us and live in us. This is what we mean by the organic union, an organic oneness in life.

BELIEVING INTO CHRIST
AND BEING BAPTIZED INTO HIM

In order to experience this organic union with the Triune God, we need to believe into Christ and be baptized into Him. Believing and being baptized are two parts of one step. First we believe into Christ, then we are baptized into Him. The Greek preposition, *eis,* used in John 3:16, 18, and 36, means into. These verses indicate that we need to believe into the Son. By believing in Christ we enter into Christ. We believe ourselves *into* Him. We have seen that M. R. Vincent says that this Greek preposition, as used in Matthew 28:19, implies a mystical, spiritual union with the Triune God. Chinese people may believe Confucius, but they would never say that they believe into Confucius. Neither would Greeks claim to believe into Plato. Chinese do not become one with Confucius, and Greeks do not enter into a spiritual union with Plato. But when we believe into the Lord Jesus, we experience an organic union with Him. When we believe in Him, we believe into Him and thereby become one spirit with Him. This is what we mean by the expression *organic union.*

In addition to believing into Christ, which is inward and subjective, we also need to be baptized into Him, an act which is outward and objective. We need both the inward action of believing and the outward action of being baptized. In this way we make one complete step to enter into the Triune God. In Galatians 3 Paul speaks often about faith and believing. But at the end of the chapter, he speaks of being baptized into Christ. The step which begins with believing into Christ is completed by being baptized into Him. In this way there takes place in full an organic union between the believers and the Triune God.

PUTTING ON CHRIST AND ONE IN CHRIST

Having been baptized into Christ, we must now put on Christ. To put on Christ is to live Christ. It is vital for Christians to realize that we need to put on Christ and live Him. According to Romans 13:14, we live Christ by putting on Christ.

To put on Christ is to clothe ourselves with Christ. Whenever we clothe ourselves in a certain way, we indicate that we intend to live in that way. In like manner, to put on Christ means that we live by Christ, in Christ, and with Christ. In particular, it means that we live out Christ. Christ becomes the expression of our living. Immediately after we have been put into Christ and have entered into an organic union with Him, we need to live Christ, to put Christ on in our living. Day by day, we need to be clothed with Christ and express Him as we live in Him, by Him, and with Him.

In 3:28 Paul says that we "are all one in Christ Jesus." This refers to the church life, the one Body, the one new man.

In 3:27 and 28 there are three crucial points. The first is that we enter into Christ; the second is that we put on Christ and express Christ by living Him; and the third is that we have the church life, where, in the one new man, the one Body, we are all one in Christ. If we have these three matters, God's eternal purpose will be fulfilled, and the desire of God's heart will be satisfied.

The book of Galatians shows that Paul was an excellent writer. After so much argument and debate in chapter three, Paul concludes by saying that we have been baptized into Christ, that we have put on Christ, and that we are all one in Christ. We who have the hearing of faith have been put into Christ. Now we need to live Christ and express Christ. This will cause us to be one in Christ in the church life.

The Galatian believers were foolish in going back to the law. Paul seemed to be telling them, "You have all been baptized into Christ and into the one Body. Now you should take Christ as your clothing, your expression, and live Him. Don't go back to the law to try to fulfill its requirements. Stay with Christ and live out Christ. Remember, you are members of the one Body, of the one new man. Stay with all those who are in Christ, and practice the church life so that God's purpose can be fulfilled. If you go back to the law, you will be in slavery again. The desire of God's heart cannot be satisfied by your efforts to keep the law. It can be satisfied only if you remain with Christ and live Him out." Praise the Lord that we have entered into an organic union with Him and that now we are living Christ in the church, the one Body. Surely this satisfies God.

SOME CRUCIAL POINTS

In this message we shall consider 4:1-7, where we see that the Spirit of sonship replaces the custody of the law. The introduction and conclusion of the book of Galatians are found, respectively, in 1:1-5 and in 6:18. In 1:6—4:31 we see the revelation of the Apostle's gospel. Then in 5:1—6:17 we see the walk of God's children. In 1:6—4:31 there are a number of crucial points. Here we see that God's Son is versus man's religion (1:6—2:10), that Christ replaces law

(2:11-21), and that the Spirit by faith is versus the flesh by law (3:1—4:31). In 3:1-14 we see that the Spirit is the blessing of the promise by faith in Christ; in 3:15-29, that the law is the custodian of the heirs of the promise; in 4:1-7 that the Spirit of sonship replaces the custody of the law; in 4:8-20, the necessity that Christ be formed in the heirs of promise; and in 4:21-31, that the children according to Spirit are versus the children according to flesh.

Chapter three of Galatians covers two main points. The first is that the Spirit is the blessing of the gospel. The second is that the law is the custodian which keeps God's children. We need to ask ourselves whether we prefer the blessing or the custodian. If we have been properly enlightened by this book, we shall certainly choose the Spirit, who is the processed Triune God. In 4:1-7 Paul continues the thought of chapter three. Here he seeks to make clear that the Spirit of sonship replaces the custody of the law.

THE TIME APPOINTED OF THE FATHER

Galatians 4:1 says, "But I say, as long as the heir is a child, he does not differ at all from a slave, though he is lord of all." The Greek word for child here means infant, minor. In verse 2 Paul continues, "But he is under guardians and stewards until the time appointed of the father." The guardians are the wardens, and the stewards are the administrators. This describes the functions of the law in God's economy. The time the Father appointed is the time of the New Testament, beginning with the first coming of Christ.

In verse 3 Paul says, "So also we, when we were children, were kept in slavery under the elements of the world." The "elements of the world" refer to the elementary principles, the rudimentary teachings of the law. The same expression is used in Colossians 2:8, where it refers to the rudimentary teachings of both Jews and Gentiles, consisting of ritualistic observances in meats, drinks, washings, and asceticism.

SONSHIP — THE FOCAL POINT
OF GOD'S ECONOMY

In verses 4 and 5 Paul goes on to say, "But when the fullness of the time came, God sent forth His Son, come of a woman, come under law, that He might redeem those under law, that we might receive the sonship." The fullness of time in verse 4 denotes the completion of the Old Testament time, which occurred at the time appointed of the Father (v. 2). In this verse Paul describes the Son as "come of a woman, come under law." The woman is, of course, the virgin Mary (Luke 1:27-35). The Son of God came of her to be the seed of woman, as promised in Genesis 3:15. Furthermore, Christ was born under law, as revealed in Luke 2:21-24, 27, and He kept the law, as the four Gospels reveal.

God's chosen people were shut up by law under its custody (3:23). Christ was born under law in order to redeem them from its custody that they might receive the sonship and become the sons of God. Hence, they should not return to the custody of law to be under its slavery as the Galatians had been seduced to do, but should remain in the sonship of God to enjoy the life supply of the Spirit in Christ. According to the entire revelation of the New Testament, God's economy is to produce sons. Sonship is the focal point of God's economy, God's dispensation. God's economy is the dispensation of Himself into His chosen people to make them His sons. Christ's redemption is to bring us into the sonship of God that we may enjoy the divine life. It is not God's economy to make us keepers of law, obeying the commandments and ordinances of the law, which was given only for a temporary purpose. God's economy is to make us sons of God, inheriting the blessing of God's promise, which was given for His eternal purpose. His eternal purpose is to have many sons for His corporate expression (Heb. 2:10; Rom. 8:29). Hence, He predestinated us unto sonship (Eph. 1:5) and regenerated us to be His sons (John 1:12-13). We should remain in His sonship that we may become His heirs to inherit all He has

planned for His eternal expression, and should not be
distracted to Judaism by the appreciation of law.

It is difficult to give an adequate definition of sonship.
Sonship involves life, maturity, position, and privilege. To
be a son of the Father, we need to have the Father's life.
However, we must go on to mature in this life. Life and
maturity give us the right, the privilege, the position, to inherit the things of the Father. According to the New Testament, sonship includes life, maturity, position, and
right.

THE SPIRIT OF THE SON

In 4:6 Paul declares, "And because you are sons, God
sent forth the Spirit of His Son into our hearts, .crying,
Abba, Father!" God's Son is the embodiment of the divine
life (1 John 5:12). Hence, the Spirit of God's Son is the
Spirit of life (Rom. 8:2). God gives us His Spirit of life, not
because we are law-keepers, but because we are His sons.
As law-keepers, we have no right to enjoy God's Spirit of
life. As the sons of God, we have the position with the full
right to participate in the Spirit of God, who has the bountiful supply of life. Such a Spirit, the Spirit of the Son of
God, is the focus of the blessing of God's promise to Abraham (3:14).

In verses 4 through 6 the Triune God is producing many
sons for the fulfillment of His eternal purpose. God the
Father sent forth God the Son to redeem us from the law
that we might receive sonship. He also sent forth God the
Spirit to impart His life into us that we might become His
sons in reality.

Basically sonship is a matter of life. The position and
the right depend on the life. In order for us to enjoy God's
sonship, we need the Spirit. Apart from the Spirit, we cannot be born of God to have the divine life. Once we have
been born of the Spirit, we need the Spirit in order to grow
in life. Without the Spirit, we cannot have the position,
right, or privilege of sonship. All the crucial points regarding sonship depend on the Spirit. By the Spirit, we have
the divine birth and the divine life. Through the Spirit we

grow unto maturity. Because of the Spirit we have the position, right, and privilege of sonship. Thus, without the Spirit sonship is vain, an empty term. But when the Spirit comes, the sonship is made real. We fully realize God's sonship in life, maturity, position, and right. The Spirit of sonship cannot be replaced by anything. On the contrary, everything, the law in particular, must be replaced by the Spirit of sonship.

Paul's concept is that the law was a custodian, a warden. Although the law could keep us in ward, it could not give us the life, maturity, position, and right of sonship. The law cannot bestow a position upon a child. It can only serve as a child conductor. The Spirit, in contrast, gives life, maturity, position, and right. Therefore, the law should not replace the Spirit; the Spirit must replace the law.

Since the law could not produce the reality of sonship, you may be wondering why the Spirit was not sent forth earlier. Why did the Spirit not come before the law? The answer is that the promise given to Abraham needed a period of time in order to be fulfilled. Although God is not slow, He waited two thousand years before sending His Son to fulfill the promise. Actually, God did not act quickly even in giving the promise. He did not come in immediately after Adam's fall to give to Adam the promise He eventually gave to Abraham. Yes, the promise was given in Genesis 3 that the seed of the woman would crush the head of the serpent. However, God waited until man's cursed and fallen situation had been fully exposed at Babel before He intervened, called out Abraham, and made a promise to him. At Babel, mankind became confounded, confused, and divided, fully exposed as being under the curse. With such a background, no doubt Abraham deeply appreciated God's promise. Abraham appreciated this promise more than Adam would have appreciated it, had the promise been given to him immediately after the fall. Therefore, the reason for the delay is found on man's side, not on God's side.

The principle is the same with respect to the fulfillment of the promise in the coming of Christ. Suppose Christ had come immediately after the promise was given to Abraham. If such had been the case, the fulfillment of the promise would not have been nearly as meaningful. Consider all that happened between the time of Abraham and the birth of the Lord Jesus. During the course of this period of two thousand years, God's chosen people were fully exposed. On the one hand, the law exposed their corruption and helplessness; on the other hand, the law kept them until the coming of Christ. The law fulfilled a necessary and useful function in keeping the children of Israel for God. The law preserved God's chosen people even while it was exposing them.

THE FULLNESS OF THE TIME

In 4:4 we see that God sent forth His Son when the fullness of the time had come. Christ came at exactly the right time. Earlier would have been too soon, and later would have been too late. Christ came when the time was right. This is illustrated by the picking of ripened fruit from a tree. If the fruit is picked too soon, it will be unripe. But if it is picked too late, it will be overripe. Christ came at the appointed time, at the fullness of time. For this reason, His coming was full of meaning.

TWO SENDINGS

In verses 4 and 6 we read of two kinds of sendings. In verse 4 Paul says that God sent forth His Son, and in verse 6, that God sent forth the Spirit of His Son. According to the promise in Genesis 3:15, Christ came under law as the seed of the woman in order to redeem those who were under law, that they might receive the sonship. The goal of Christ's redemption is not heaven, as many Christians believe; it is sonship. Christ redeemed us so that we may have God's sonship. Through His redemption, He has opened the way for us to possess the sonship. However, if the Spirit had not come, our sonship would be empty. It would be a sonship in position or form, not a sonship with reality. The reality of sonship, which depends on life and maturity, comes only by the Spirit. Therefore, verse 6 declares that God has sent forth the Spirit of His Son into our hearts.

We should not believe that the Spirit of the Son is a person separate from the Son. Actually, the Spirit of the Son is another form of the Son. We have pointed out that the One who was crucified on the cross was Christ, but the One who enters into the believers is the Spirit. In crucifixion for our redemption, this One was Christ, but in the indwelling to be our life, He is the Spirit. When the Son died on the cross, He was Christ, but when He enters into us, He is the Spirit. First He came as the Son under the law to qualify us for sonship and to open the way for us to share in the sonship. But after He had finished this work, He became, in resurrection, the life-giving Spirit and comes to us as the Spirit of the Son. Thus, first God the Father sent the Son to accomplish redemption and to qualify us for sonship. Then He sent the Spirit to vitalize the sonship and to make it real in our experience. Today sonship actually depends upon the Spirit of God's Son.

THE SPIRIT IN OUR HEARTS

In verse 6 Paul says that God sent forth the Spirit of His Son into our hearts. Actually the Spirit of God came into our spirit at our regeneration (John 3:6; Rom. 8:16). Because our spirit is hidden in our heart (1 Pet. 3:4), and because the word here refers to a matter that is related to our feeling and understanding, both of which belong to our heart, it says that the Spirit of God's Son was sent into our heart.

Romans 8:15 is a verse that is parallel to Galatians 4:6. Romans 8:15 says that we who have received a spirit of sonship cry, in this spirit, Abba, Father, whereas Galatians 4:6 says that the Spirit of God's Son is crying in our heart, Abba, Father. This indicates that our regenerated spirit and the Spirit of God are mingled as one, and that our spirit is in our heart. This also indicates that with us the sonship of God is realized by our subjective experience in the depths of our being. In this verse Paul appeals to such an experience of the Galatian believers for his revelation. This appeal is quite convincing and subduing, not merely because of the objective doctrines, but because of the experiential facts.

Abba is an Aramaic word, thus a Hebrew word, and Father is the translation of the Greek word *pater*. Such a term was first used by the Lord Jesus in Gethsemane while praying to the Father (Mark 14:36). The combination of the Hebrew title with the Greek expresses a stronger affection in crying to the Father. Such an affectionate cry implies an intimate relationship in life between a genuine son and a begetting father.

As humans we have not only a spirit, but we also have our person, our being. The center of our person is our heart. For us to become sons of God not only involves our spirit, but also involves our heart as the center of our personality. The New Testament clearly reveals that the spirit is in the heart (1 Pet. 3:4). Therefore, it is not possible for the Spirit to be sent into our spirit without also being sent into our heart. It is important for us to realize that our spirit is the kernel, the central part, of our heart. When God's Spirit was sent into our spirit, the Spirit was sent into the kernel of our heart. When the Spirit cries within us, He cries from our spirit and through our heart. Hence, concerning sonship, our heart must be involved.

The inner sense we have as we call on the Lord from our spirit through our heart is mainly in the heart, not in the spirit. This implies that to be genuinely spiritual we need to be emotional in a proper way. Brother Nee once said that a person who cannot laugh or cry cannot be truly spiritual. We are not senseless statues; we are human beings with feelings. Therefore, the more we cry, Abba, Father, in the spirit, the deeper will be the sweet and intimate sense in our heart.

The sense we have when calling in this way is sweet and

intimate. Although the Spirit of sonship has come into our spirit, the Spirit cries in our hearts, Abba, Father. This indicates that our relationship with our Father in the sonship is sweet and very intimate. For example, when a son calls his father "Daddy," there may be a sweet and intimate sense deep within. However, the sense is not the same if he tries to say the same thing to his father-in-law. The reason is that with the father-in-law there is no relationship in life. But how sweet it is when little children, enjoying a relationship in life with their fathers, say tenderly, "Daddy." In like manner, how tender and sweet it is to call God, Abba, Father! Such an intimate calling involves our emotion as well as our spirit. The Spirit of sonship in our spirit cries, Abba, Father, from our heart. This proves that we have a genuine, bona fide relationship in life with our Father. We are His real sons.

NO LONGER SLAVES, BUT SONS

Since we have the Spirit of sonship, we no longer need to be held under the custody of the law. We do not need the law to be our guardian, steward, or child-conductor. In 4:7 Paul says, "So you are no longer a slave, but a son; and if a son, an heir also through God." The New Testament believer is no longer a slave to works under law, but a son in life under grace. Instead of the law to keep us in custody, we have the all-inclusive Spirit. This Spirit is everything to us. Whereas the law could not give life, the Spirit gives life and brings us into maturity that we may have the full position and right of sons. The custody of the law has been replaced by the Spirit of sonship.

HEIRS THROUGH GOD

As sons, we are also heirs through God. An heir is one who is of full age according to the law (the Roman law is used for illustration) and who is qualified to inherit the Father's estate. The New Testament believers become heirs of God not through the law or through their fleshly father, but through God, even the Triune God — the

Father who sent forth the Son and the Spirit (vv. 4, 6), the Son who accomplished redemption for sonship (v. 5), and the Spirit who carries out the sonship within us (v. 6).

LIFE-STUDY OF GALATIANS

MESSAGE TWENTY-THREE

THE NEED FOR CHRIST TO BE FORMED IN THE HEIRS OF PROMISE

Scripture Reading: Gal. 4:8-20

In this message we shall consider 4:8-20. These verses indicate that the Apostle Paul was in a difficult situation with respect to the believers in Galatia. They had been brought to the Lord through Paul's preaching of the gospel, and he had a heart to care for them. Paul's burden was not to carry on a Christian work, but was to minister Christ to the believers, to labor that Christ might be formed in them (v. 19). It is possible to work for the Lord and to help the saints, without having the burden to minister Christ to them. We may earnestly work for Christ without having any burden to see Christ formed in the saints. Hence, it is important for us to see that Paul's burden as expressed in these verses was altogether different from that of most Christian workers. We may be burdened for the raising up of local churches and for the strengthening of the churches. However, we may not have the burden to minister Christ into the saints. To preach the gospel and raise up churches is one thing; to bear the burden to minister Christ into the saints is another. Paul's burden was not for a work; it was for ministering Christ into the believers. This is the reason that in 4:8-20 Paul uses certain intimate expressions, expressions which show the closeness of his relationship to the Galatian believers and his affection for them. Let us now consider 4:8-20 verse by verse.

ENSLAVED AND DECEIVED

Verse 8 says, "But then indeed, not knowing God, you were slaves to the gods which by nature do not exist." The gods, or the idols, do not have the divine nature. They were considered gods by their superstitious worshippers, but by nature they do not exist as gods.

In verse 9 Paul says, "But now, knowing God, but rather being known by God, how is it that you turn again to the weak and poor elements, to which you desire to be again enslaved?" The "elements" here are not substances. They are the elementary principles of the law, its rudimentary teachings. Here Paul points out that by turning again to the weak and poor elements of the law, the Galatian believers would once again become enslaved. Paul's use of the word enslaved indicates how serious the Judaizers were in working on the Galatian believers. The Judaizers bewitched them, deceived them, to such a degree that they were brought into slavery. To the Judaizers, the law was a matter of life and death. Therefore, they were desperate in their attempt to mislead the Galatians. Paul realized that once the Galatian believers had been deceived, they would be enslaved. To say that the Galatians were enslaved means that they had been deceived to the uttermost.

RELIGIOUS OBSERVANCES

In verse 10 Paul continues, "You observe days and months and seasons and years." The observances here were Jewish religious observances. The days mentioned were the Sabbaths and new moons (Isa. 66:23). The months were the sacred months like the first, Abib, the ear-month (Exo. 13:4); the second, Zif, the flower-month (1 Kings 6:1, 37); the seventh, Ethanim, the month of streaming rivers (1 Kings 8:2); and the eighth, Bul, the month of rain (1 Kings 6:38). The seasons were festal seasons such as the Passover, Pentecost, and the Feast of Tabernacles (2 Chron. 8:13). The years perhaps denoted sabbatical years (Lev. 25:4).

In verse 11 Paul tells the Galatians, "I fear for you, lest I have labored upon you in vain." Paul labored upon the Galatians to bring them into Christ under grace. Their turning to the Jewish religious observances might cause Paul's labor upon them to be in vain. It seems Paul was telling the believers in Galatia, "I labored on you and ministered Christ into you. Why, after receiving what I ministered to you, would you go back to the ordinances of the law?" Paul was puzzled. He simply could not believe that those who had received his preaching could be bewitched to such a degree that they would return to the observances of the law and become enslaved to them.

BECOMING AS PAUL WAS

Verse 12 says, "Become as I am, because I also am as you, brothers, I beseech you. You did not injure me at all. " Paul was free from the bondage of Jewish observances. He besought the Galatians to become as he was, even as he had become as a Gentile for the truth of the gospel. Having done his best to become the same as the Galatians, he now besought them to become as he is. He seemed to be saying, "I love you and became like you. Now I ask you to become as I am. I am not for days, months, seasons, and years. I am for Christ. I beg you, become as I am."

In verse 12 Paul tells the Galatians that they did not injure him at all. The Galatians had not injured Paul in the past. Paul expects that neither would they injure him now.

AN OPPORTUNITY TO MINISTER CHRIST

Verse 13 continues, "And you know that on account of weakness of the flesh I preached the gospel to you formerly." In his first journey, Paul was detained in Galatia because of physical weakness. While there, he preached the gospel to the Galatians. His illness afforded him a good opportunity to minister Christ to them.

Verse 14 says, "And that which was a trial to you in my flesh you did not despise nor loathe, but you received me as a messenger of God, as Christ Jesus." Here Paul appeals to their love by reminding them that they had received him as a messenger of God, an angel, and had not despised his sickness.

THEIR BLESSEDNESS

In verse 15 Paul goes on to say, "Where then is your blessedness? For I testify to you that if possible you would have torn out your eyes and given them to me." The Greek words rendered "your blessedness" also mean your felicitation, your happiness. The Galatians formerly considered Paul's being retained in their place and preaching the gospel to them a blessing. They were happy about it and boasted of it. That became their felicitation. However, now that they had departed from Paul's preaching of the gospel, the apostle questions them, "Where then is your blessedness, your happiness, your felicitation?"

When Paul was among them, the Galatians celebrated their happiness with one another and congratulated one another for the opportunity to have such a minister of Christ with them. When Paul was in Galatia preaching the gospel, ministering Christ to the people, they were happy and regarded Paul's presence as a great blessing. This happiness, blessedness, felicitation, is what is implied by the Greek term used here.

The Galatians appreciated Paul's preaching and loved him to such an extent that, as he says, if possible, they would have torn out their eyes and given them to him. This may indicate that Paul's physical weakness (v. 13) was in his eyes. This may be confirmed by the large letters he used in writing to them (6:11). It may also be the thorn in his flesh, some physical weakness, which he prayed might be removed from him (2 Cor. 12:7-9).

AN APPEAL TO THE BELIEVERS' AFFECTION

In verse 16 Paul asks, "So have I become your enemy in speaking the truth to you?" This word indicates that certain of the deceived ones had come to regard Paul as an enemy. Suppose some brothers visit the saints in a certain region, and the saints there receive them gladly. However, later the saints are distracted by some teaching or practice and turn against the very brothers whom they once gladly received and appreciated highly. In such a case, these brothers may be tempted to give up on the saints in that region. But this definitely was not Paul's attitude. On the contrary, he was burdened to write them and to appeal to them in a loving manner. We should learn of Paul to take up the burden for those believers who have turned away from us. Perhaps we should write them and say, "Do you not remember how you served us in love? Where is your love today? It seems that now you consider us your enemies. To be sure, this is not reasonable. Are we enemies simply because we speak the truth to you?"

In writing Galatians 3, Paul spoke like an attorney. But in composing chapter four, he wrote like a loving father. Chapter four was written according to Paul's personal and intimate love for the Galatians. Instead of arguing in a legal way like a lawyer, Paul appealed to the believers' affection. If we would be those who minister Christ to others, we must learn to speak to them in such a way. We should not simply speak according to doctrinal truth, but should appeal to others in a personal, loving manner.

THE AIM OF THE JUDAIZERS

Verse 17 says, "They are zealous of you, not rightly, but they desire to shut you out, that you may be zealous of them." The Greek word rendered zealous in this verse means to be jealously courting someone. The Judaizers were jealously courting the Galatians so that the Galatians might jealously court them in return. To court a person is to pursue that person in love with the aim of gaining his love. The Judaizers pursued the Galatian believers in this way, actually courting them. This indicates how serious, how zealous, the Judaizers were. However, as Paul says, the Judaizers jealously courted them, not rightly, but with the desire to shut them out. They did not pursue them in an honorable, commendable way. Their aim was to exclude them from the proper preaching of the gospel of grace. They wanted to exclude them from God's New Testament economy, from the enjoyment of Christ, and from the all-inclusive life-giving Spirit. The principle is the same with dissenting ones today. Their goal is to shut out the church people from the enjoyment of Christ and to cause the ones they have deceived to zealously follow them.

In verse 18 Paul continues, "But it is good always to be zealous in a good thing, and not only when I am present with you." It is good to jealously court someone in a good thing, in the proper preaching of the gospel. This should be the case not only when Paul is present. By this word Paul indicates that he is not narrow, keeping other preachers of the gospel away from the Galatians. Rather, he rejoices in the preaching of others (Phil. 1:18). Paul was in favor of the proper preaching of others, but he was not in favor of that kind of jealous courting of the believers.

PAUL'S TRAVAIL

Verse 19 says, "My children, of whom I am again in travail until Christ is formed in you." Here Paul considers himself the begetting father, and the Galatian believers his children begotten of him in Christ (see 1 Cor. 4:15; Philem. 10). This also was an appeal to their affection.

Paul told the Galatian believers that he was again travailing on their behalf. Travail refers to painful labor in childbirth. In this metaphor Paul likens himself to a mother who gives birth to a child. He labored in this way for the regeneration of the Galatians when he first preached the gospel to them. Because they had deviated from the gospel he preached to them, he labors again in travail until Christ is formed in them. In this verse Paul likens himself both to a begetting father and a travailing mother. Was he, then, a father or a mother? He was both, depending on the situation. On one occasion he was a begetting father; on another, a travailing mother.

Paul was in travail that Christ might be formed in the Galatians. Christ, a living Person, is the focus of Paul's gospel. His preaching is to bring forth Christ, the Son of the living God, in the believers. This differs greatly from the teaching of the law in letters. Hence, the book of Galatians is emphatically Christ-centered. Christ was crucified (3:1) to redeem us out of the curse of the law (3:13) and rescue us out of the evil religious course of the world (1:4); and He was resurrected from among the dead (1:1) that He might live in us (2:20). We were baptized into Him, identified with Him, and have put on Him, have clothed ourselves with Him (3:27). Thus, we are in Him (3:28) and have become His (3:29; 5:24). On the other hand, He has been revealed in us (1:16), He is now living in us (2:20), and He will be formed in us (4:19). It is to Him the law has conducted us (3:24), and in Him we are all sons of God (3:26). It is in Him that we inherit God's promised blessing and enjoy the all-inclusive Spirit (3:14). It is also in Him that we are all one (3:28). We should not be deprived of all profit from Him and so be severed from Him (5:4). We need Him to supply us with His grace in our spirit (6:18) that we may live Him.

Christ was born into the Galatian believers, but not formed in them, when they were regenerated through Paul's preaching the gospel to them the first time. Now the apostle travails again that Christ might be formed in them. To have Christ formed in us is to have Christ grown in us in full. First Christ was born into us at our conversion, then He lives in us in our Christian life (2:20), and He will be formed in us at our maturity. This is needed that we may be sons of full age, heirs to inherit God's promised blessing, and mature in the divine sonship.

MINISTERING CHRIST

As we have indicated, verse 19 points out that Paul's burden was not to carry on a Christian work, but was to have Christ formed in the believers. Through Paul's preaching, Christ had entered into the Galatians. But because they had been deceived, Christ had not yet grown in them and had not been formed in them. Therefore, Paul labored again, like a mother laboring in giving birth, that Christ would be formed in the believers. Paul wrote out of

206 of LIFE-STUDY OF GALATIANS

the burden to minister Christ into the saints. He was burdened that Christ would be established, built up, in them. Galatians tells us that Christ is revealed in us and that He lives in us. Now we see that Christ must also be formed in us.

Ministering Christ to others is not accomplished easily. It often requires suffering and struggle. Ministering Christ is much more difficult than carrying on an ordinary Christian work. If you would bear the burden, with a sincere heart, to minister Christ to others, you will discover what labor and suffering it requires. You will need to labor like a mother giving birth to a child.

The goal of our service in the church or in the ministry must be to minister Christ into others. It is not adequate simply to say that we preach the gospel, for it is possible to preach the gospel without ministering Christ to others. Our burden must be the ministering of Christ. Once again I say that this requires labor and suffering. It demands prayer, patience, and love. According to our experience, such a ministry is a battle, a wrestling. The subtle one, the enemy of God, is active to bring in frustration or distraction. We do not know from what direction he will attack next. Hence, we must learn from Paul to be burdened to minister Christ and also to appeal to the saints' affection that their hearts may be touched.

PAUL'S PERPLEXITY

In verse 20 Paul says, "And I wished to be present with you now and to change my tone, because I am perplexed about you." The apostle wanted to change his tone from severity to affection, as a mother speaking lovingly to her children. Paul was puzzled in dealing with the Galatians. He was searching for the best way to recover them from their deviation from Christ.

Verse 20 indicates that Paul felt that what he had written to the Galatian believers was not adequate. He wanted to visit them and stay with them because he knew that his presence would accomplish more than his writing.

Paul was perplexed about the Galatians; he did not know how to deal with them, how to handle their case. On the one hand, he addressed them as "foolish Galatians"; on the other hand, he appealed to them as "beloved brothers." This indicates that Paul was perplexed.

THE NEED TO BE PURE IN MOTIVE

In writing chapter four Paul was very affectionate and appealed to the affection of the Galatian believers. It is very difficult to appeal to others' personal affection in a proper way. To do this requires that our motive be pure. If we are not pure in our motive, we should be careful of our affection for the saints. There is a great need of affectionate contact with the saints; there is also the need to appeal to the affection of others. However, we must recognize that such an appeal is difficult, for it is easy for the natural love, the "honey," to be present. It is not easy to be pure as Paul was in Galatians 4. Paul was a person who had been "salted." This was the reason that he could appeal to the Galatians' personal affection in such a pure way. He could even rebuke them and condemn the Judaizers with a pure intent. If we try to practice this, we shall discover how difficult it is. In rebuking others we need a pure motive. In appealing to others' personal affection, we need to be even more pure in our motive. In many situations we shall not be able to minister Christ to others, to travail to have Christ formed in them, if we are not able to appeal to their affection.

As we consider all these points, we see that chapter four is as important as chapter three. I thank the Lord that Paul wrote this chapter. Otherwise, we might have the impression that in writing to the Galatians he was legal, but not personal or affectionate. In chapter four Paul could be affectionate and appeal to the love of the saints for the purpose of ministering Christ to them.

LIFE-STUDY OF GALATIANS

MESSAGE TWENTY-FOUR

TWO COVENANTS AND TWO KINDS OF CHILDREN

Scripture Reading: Gal. 4:21-31; 2:20a; 6:12-13, 15

In the previous message we pointed out that in 4:19 Paul says, "My children, of whom I am again in travail until Christ is formed in you." If we consider this verse in its context, we see that it is necessary for the heirs of the promise to have Christ formed in them. Those who are sons of Abraham through faith are the heirs of the promise, those who inherit the blessing. These heirs need to be filled, occupied, and saturated with Christ. They need to have Christ formed in them.

PERMEATED AND SATURATED WITH CHRIST

If we would know what it means for Christ to be formed in us, we need to consider not only the entire book of Galatians, but also the books of Ephesians, Philippians, and Colossians. The book of Galatians indicates that God's intention is for Christ to be wrought into His chosen people that they may become sons of God. In order to be God's sons, we need to be permeated and saturated with Christ. Christ must occupy our entire being. The Galatians, however, were distracted from Christ to the law. Hence, Paul told them repeatedly that it was altogether wrong to leave Christ and return to the law. The believers should come back to Christ, who is both the seed who fulfills God's promise to Abraham and also the good land, the all-inclusive Spirit to be our enjoyment. As believers, we need the full enjoyment of this blessing, the full enjoyment of the life-giving Spirit. We need to be permeated, saturated, possessed, and fully taken over by this Spirit and

with this Spirit. According to the context of the book of
Galatians, to have Christ formed in us is to allow Him to
permeate our being and to saturate our inward parts.
When Christ occupies our inner being in this way, He is
formed in us.

OCCUPIED BY THE ALL-INCLUSIVE SPIRIT

In order to have Christ formed in us, we need to drop
everything other than Christ Himself, no matter how good
these things may be. Even things which come from God
and are scriptural may not be Christ Himself. Although
the law was given by God, it must be set aside so that
all the ground in our being may be given over to Christ. We
need to allow Him to saturate every part of our inner being.
He must occupy us and saturate our mind, emotion, and
will. To have Christ possess our entire being is to have Him
formed in us.

In Ephesians 3:17 we see that Paul prayed that "Christ
may make His home in your hearts." We know that the
heart includes the mind, the will, the emotion, and the
conscience. To let Christ make His home in our hearts
means that He makes His home in all these parts of our
inner being. If Christ is to make home in our hearts, He
needs to be able to settle down within us. Once again, this
is to have Christ formed in us.

To have Christ formed in us is to allow the all-inclusive
Spirit to occupy every part of our inner being. The law
should not have any room in our mind, emotion, or will. All
the ground within us must be for Christ. We need to allow
Christ to occupy us fully. He should not only spread into
our mind, emotion, and will; He should actually become
our mind, emotion, and will. Let Christ be your thought,
decision, and love. Let Him be everything to you. This is to
have Christ formed in you. Everything other than Christ
must diminish, and Christ must become everything to us
in our experience.

THE FULL ENJOYMENT
OF THE BLESSING OF THE GOSPEL

Christ today is the life-giving Spirit as the blessing of the gospel, the blessing promised by God. To have the full enjoyment of this blessing is to let Christ be formed in us. This means that if we would have the full enjoyment of the blessing of the gospel, we need to have Christ formed in us. If Christ is not yet fully formed in us, then our enjoyment of the blessing of the New Testament is not yet full. Although we have enjoyed the blessing in part, we need to go on to allow Christ to occupy us wholly, to take us over and saturate every part of our being with Himself. To do this is to enjoy the blessing of the gospel to the uttermost. This was Paul's goal in writing to the Galatian believers. As He appealed to their personal affection in 4:8-20, Paul had this goal clearly in mind. He appealed to the believers' affection so that Christ might be formed in them for the fulfillment of God's goal.

Galatians 4:21 says, "Tell me, you who desire to be under the law, do you not hear the law?" The book of Galatians deals strongly with deviation from Christ by coming back under the law. Such deviation shuts the believers out from the enjoyment of Christ as their life and their everything.

TWO SONS

We have seen that in 4:8-20 Paul spoke in an affectionate manner and appealed to the personal feeling of the Galatians. He did this for the purpose of ministering Christ to them. But in verse 21 Paul goes back to the tone he used in chapter three. In fact, he speaks to them in an even stronger way. In verses 22 and 23 Paul continues, "For it is written that Abraham had two sons, one of the maidservant and one of the free woman. But the one of the maidservant was born according to flesh, and the one of the free woman through the promise." To be born according to flesh is to be born by man's fleshly effort, whereas to be born through the promise is to be born through God's power in grace, which is implied in His promise. Ishmael was born in the former way, but Isaac in the latter. According to the context, the law goes with the flesh, and grace goes with the promise. The child born of the maidservant was born according to the flesh, whereas the one born of the free woman was born according to grace. Because grace goes with the promise, to be born through promise is to be born through grace.

TWO WOMEN

Speaking of the two women in verse 22, Paul says in verse 24, "Which things are an allegory; for these are two covenants, one from Mount Sinai, bringing forth children unto slavery, which is Hagar. Now this Hagar is Mount Sinai in Arabia, and corresponds to the Jerusalem which now is, for she is in slavery with her children." Of the two covenants mentioned in verse 24, one is the covenant of promise to Abraham, which is related to the New Testament, the covenant of grace, and the other is the covenant of law related to Moses, which has nothing to do with the New Testament. Sarah, the free woman, represents the covenant of promise, and Hagar, the maidservant, the covenant of law.

Mount Sinai was the place where the law was given (Exo. 19:20). The slavery spoken of in verse 24 is the slavery under the law. Hagar, the concubine of Abraham, signifies the law. Hence, the position of the law is like that of a concubine. Sarah, the wife of Abraham, symbolizes the grace of God (John 1:17), which has the right position in God's economy. The law, like Hagar, brought forth children unto slavery like the Judaizers. Grace, like Sarah, brings forth children unto sonship. These are the New Testament believers. They are no longer under law, but under grace (Rom. 6:14). They should stand in this grace (Rom. 5:2) and not fall from it (Gal. 5:4).

In verse 25 Paul mentions "the Jerusalem which now is." Jerusalem, as the choice of God (1 Kings 14:21; Psa.

48:2, 8), should belong to the covenant of promise represented by Sarah. However, because it brings God's chosen people into the bondage of law, it corresponds to Mount Sinai, which belongs to the covenant of law represented by Hagar. Jerusalem and her children were slaves under the law at Paul's time.

Paul's word in verses 24 and 25 was clear and strong. No doubt, the Judaizers must have been offended by it.

Verse 26 says, "But the Jerusalem above is free, who is our mother." The mother of the Judaizers is the earthly Jerusalem, but the mother of believers is the heavenly Jerusalem. This will eventually be the New Jerusalem in the new heaven and new earth (Rev. 21:1-2), which is related to the covenant of promise. She is the mother of the New Testament believers, who are not slaves under law, but sons under grace. We, the New Testament believers, are all born of her from above.

ABRAHAM'S DESCENDANTS

Verse 27 goes on to say, "For it is written, Rejoice, barren one who does not bear; break forth and shout, you who are not travailing, because many are the children of the desolate rather than of her who has a husband." This indicates that Abraham's spiritual descendants, who belong to the heavenly Jerusalem, to the covenant of promise under the freedom of grace, are many more than his natural descendants, who belong to the earthly Jerusalem, to the covenant of law under the slavery of law.

According to Genesis 22:17, God promised that Abraham's descendants would be like the sand of the seashore and like the stars of heaven. Here we see two kinds of descendants, the heavenly and the earthly, the spiritual and the natural. The Jews are Abraham's descendants according to the flesh, whereas the believers in Christ are his descendants according to the Spirit. The natural descendants, the Jews, are like the sand of the seashore, but the spiritual descendants, the Christians, who outnumber the natural descendants, are like the stars.

214   LIFE-STUDY OF GALATIANS

Verse 28 continues, "But you, brothers, according to Isaac, are children of promise." The children of promise are those born of the heavenly Jerusalem through grace under the covenant of promise.

ISHMAEL'S PERSECUTION OF ISAAC

Verse 29 says, "But as then he that was born according to flesh persecuted him that was born according to Spirit, so also it is now." The two kinds of children brought forth by the two covenants are different in their natures. Those brought forth by the covenant of law are born according to flesh; those brought forth by the covenant of promise are born according to Spirit. The children born according to flesh have no right to participate in God's promised blessing, but the children born according to the Spirit have the full right. The Judaizers were the former kind of children; the believers in Christ are the latter. The children of promise (v. 28) are born according to Spirit, God's Spirit of life, who is the very blessing of God's promise to Abraham (3:14).

Paul says that the one born according to flesh persecuted the one born according to the Spirit. This indicates that Ishmael persecuted Isaac (Gen. 21:9). Furthermore, the Judaizers, the descendants of Abraham according to flesh, also persecuted the believers, the descendants of Abraham according to the Spirit, as Ishmael did Isaac. The same is true today. Today's Ishmaels, those according to flesh, are persecuting the real Isaacs, the children according to the Spirit.

SONS OF ABRAHAM AND
CHILDREN OF THE FREE WOMAN

In verses 30 and 31 Paul concludes, "But what does the Scripture say? Cast out the maidservant and her son; for the son of the maidservant shall by no means inherit with the son of the free woman. Wherefore, brothers, we are not children of a maidservant, but of the free woman." The Judaizers under the slavery of law are the sons of the maidservant, who shall by no means inherit God's promised blessing — the all-inclusive Spirit. The believers of the New Testament under the freedom of grace are the sons of the free woman, who shall inherit the promised blessing of the Spirit. We, the believers in Christ, are not children of law under its slavery, but children of grace under its freedom to enjoy the all-inclusive Spirit with all the riches of Christ. It is important to remember that the free woman represents grace and the promise, whereas the maidservant, Hagar, represents the law and also the efforts of the flesh. Thus, the law brought forth children according to the flesh, but the promise and grace brought forth children according to the Spirit.

The conclusion of chapter four is very similar to that of chapter three. Paul ends chapter three by saying that we "are Abraham's seed, heirs according to promise." Then he closes chapter four with these words: "Wherefore, brothers, we are not children of a maidservant, but of the free woman." At the end of chapter three, we see that we are sons of Abraham, but at the end of chapter four, that we are children of the free woman, those who inherit the promise. Actually, these two chapters speak of the same thing viewed from different angles.

FIVE POSITIVE MATTERS

As we consider the matter of two covenants and two kinds of children, we need to be impressed with God's promise, grace, Christ, the Spirit, and the children according to Spirit. In contrast to these, we have the law, flesh, slavery, and the children according to the flesh. The children according to the flesh are those held in slavery. In this message I am burdened that we all be impressed with the five positive matters of promise, grace, Christ, the Spirit, and the children according to the Spirit.

THE UNVEILING OF GOD'S DESIRE

The promise given to Abraham was the unveiling of God's desire. When God made the promise to Abraham, He opened His heart and unveiled the desire of His heart. Although man had fallen and was under the curse, God's desire was to bless all nations. His desire was to give Himself as a blessing to the nations. God had told Abraham that in Him all nations would be blessed (Gen. 12:3). This promise was given over against a certain background. At the time the promise was given, all the nations were under the curse. No doubt, Abraham realized this. Then, suddenly, the God of glory appeared to him and promised that in him all the nations would be blessed. What a tremendous word this was! When the God of glory appeared to Abraham in Ur of the Chaldees, Abraham was attracted. He was charmed. Because he was attracted by God, Abraham could follow Him out of Chaldea. Then, when Abraham was sojourning in the land of Canaan, God promised to give the land to Abraham's seed. Therefore, with God's promise to Abraham there are two main aspects: the aspect of the nations being blessed and the aspect of the good land. On the one hand, the nations would be blessed through Christ's redemption. On the other hand, Christ, typified by the good land, is the embodiment of the Triune God as the all-inclusive life-giving Spirit as our enjoyment and bountiful supply. God's promise to Abraham with these two aspects was the unveiling of the desire of God's heart.

God's promise to Abraham involves much more than justification by faith. Yes, we are told that Abraham believed God and that it was reckoned to him as righteousness (3:6). However, we need to see that God's dealing with Abraham involved much more. The gospel preached to Abraham was actually the unveiling of God's heart.

THE COMING OF CHRIST AND OF GRACE

Two thousand years after the desire of God's heart was unveiled to Abraham, Christ came. When Christ came,

grace came. Grace is the Triune God processed to become
our enjoyment. Such a grace is the fulfillment of God's
promise, the fulfillment of God's desire.

Before the coming of Christ, we are not told in the
Scriptures that God was happy or pleased. But when
Christ was baptized, the Father declared, "This is My
beloved Son, in Whom I delight" (Matt. 3:17). When the
Lord was with three of the disciples on the mount of transfiguration, the Father spoke the same words (Matt. 17:5).
God was happy to see the fulfillment of His desire by grace,
which is actually a living Person, Christ, the Son of God,
the embodiment of the Triune God. This living Person is
the fulfillment of the desire of God's heart. It is correct to
say that the fulfillment of God's promise is both by grace
and by the living Person of Christ, for this living Person is
Himself the grace.

THE LIFE-GIVING SPIRIT

Today we are enjoying this grace, this living Person,
who is now the life-giving Spirit within us. If Christ were
not the life-giving Spirit dwelling in us, we could not be one
with Him, and it would not be possible for Him to work all
the riches of the Godhead into our being. How could Christ
live in us and be formed in us if He were only an objective
One sitting in the heavens at the right hand of the Father,
as One separate from the Father and the Spirit? It would
be impossible! Such a Christ could not be revealed into us,
live in us, or be formed in us. In order for all this to become our experience, Christ must be the life-giving Spirit.
Praise the Lord that the grace we enjoy is Christ, and
Christ is the life-giving Spirit!

CHILDREN ACCORDING TO SPIRIT

Because we have grace, Christ, and the life-giving
Spirit, we are children according to Spirit. How blessed we
are to have the hearing of faith and by it to receive grace!
We have seen that the desire of God's heart, the promise
given to Abraham, is fulfilled by grace and that grace is

Christ as the life-giving Spirit. This Spirit is now in our spirit and makes us children according to Spirit. This is the revelation in Galatians 3 and 4.

As those who are children according to Spirit, we should lay aside the law, the flesh, slavery, and the children according to flesh. We need to bid farewell to these things and refuse from now on to be entangled by them. Instead, we should remain in the fulfillment of God's desire, enjoying grace, Christ, and the all-inclusive Spirit as the blessing of the gospel.

OUR CHOICE

In 4:21-31 we see two women, two covenants, and two Jerusalems. We can choose between Hagar and Sarah, between the earthly Jerusalem and the Jerusalem above, and between the covenant of law and the covenant of promise, which is the testament of grace. Furthermore, we may choose to be children according to flesh or children according to Spirit. Praise the Lord for showing us the two covenants and the two kinds of children! Chapters three and four of Galatians are crystal clear to us, fully transparent. We praise the Lord that we are of the Jerusalem above, children of the free woman! Praise Him that we are children according to the Spirit enjoying the all-inclusive Spirit as the blessing of the gospel!